Maximizing Investment Returns

Navigating the Crypto Market:
A Comprehensive Guide to Successful
Investments

Samantha Cruz

Table of Contents

CHAPTER V: Diversification and Portfolio Management 67

CHAPTER VI: Navigating Regulatory and Security Challenges 77

CHAPTER VII: Identifying Promising Cryptocurrencies ... 89

CHAPTER VIII: Long-Term vs. Short-Term Investments... 98

INTRODUCTION

Cryptocurrencies have arisen as a revolutionary force in the financial sector in a world that is fast changing and where technology influences the way we communicate, transact, and invest. Welcome to "Maximizing Investment Returns: Navigating the Crypto Market - A Comprehensive Guide to Successful Investments." This book is an essential resource for managing the constantly changing and frequently confusing world of cryptocurrency investments.

The interest in and use of cryptocurrencies has skyrocketed during the past decade. The world of cryptocurrency has grown far beyond its original boundaries due to the groundbreaking Bitcoin, which introduced us to decentralized digital currency. A broad ecosystem of alternative coins and innovative blockchain projects followed this. Cryptocurrencies are changing how we think about money, technology, and investing opportunities. They are no longer just a specialized area of interest.

Cryptocurrencies have an undeniable attraction. These digital assets have drawn the interest of investors, entrepreneurs, and visionaries alike due to their potential for exponential returns and their promise to disrupt established financial structures. However, in addition to the possible benefits, some inherent risks and complications necessitate careful consideration.

As with every revolutionary innovation, the cryptocurrency market is filled with potential and challenges. Although liberating, cryptocurrency's decentralized structure also brings regulatory uncertainty and security issues. Another level of complexity is added by the extremely high volatility that can produce gains or losses overnight. But these difficulties offer possibilities for those who arm themselves with knowledge, strategies, and a patient mindset.

This thorough book is intended to accompany you as you make your cryptocurrency investment journey. This book is appropriate for traders of all levels, whether you are an experienced trader looking to improve your methods or a novice excited by the promise of blockchain technology. We'll cover everything, from the fundamentals of how cryptocurrencies operate to advanced investment strategies, risk management strategies, and market sentiment analysis.

As we progress through the chapters, you will develop a thorough understanding of the guiding concepts that underpin the cryptocurrency market. You'll discover how to perform thorough research, separate worthwhile endeavors from fleeting trends, and create a well-rounded investing portfolio suited to your objectives and risk tolerance. We'll go through the technical and fundamental aspects of analysis, giving you the knowledge and resources, you need to make wise choices in a market noted for its rapid shifts.

Get ready to start a journey that goes beyond the boundaries of the conventional investment environment. Those who approach the world of cryptocurrencies with knowledge and strategy will find it vibrant, disruptive, and full of opportunity. After reading this book, you'll be equipped with the information and assurance necessary to deal with the volatility of the cryptocurrency market as well as the practical skills needed to make wise investments.

So, let's get started. The world of crypto investments awaits; this book is your compass to navigate it successfully.

CHAPTER I

The Basics of Cryptocurrencies

What Are Cryptocurrencies?

In the vast realm of digital innovation, cryptocurrencies have emerged as a groundbreaking phenomenon, challenging traditional notions of currency and revolutionizing how we conduct financial transactions. At their core, cryptocurrencies are decentralized digital assets that utilize cryptographic techniques to secure and facilitate transactions within a peer-to-peer network. Cryptocurrencies work on a distributed ledger technology called blockchain, in contrast to conventional currencies that are issued and governed by central banks.

The idea of decentralization is at the core of cryptocurrencies. Cryptocurrencies work on a network of computers that jointly validate and record transactions, as opposed to relying on a single centralized authority, like a government or financial institution. This decentralized nature is fundamental to their security and resilience. A consensus mechanism verifies each transaction, ensuring transparency and eliminating the need for middlemen.

The pioneering cryptocurrency, Bitcoin, introduced by an anonymous individual or group using Satoshi Nakamoto's pseudonym in 2008, laid the foundation for this transformative technology. Bitcoin's whitepaper outlined a peer-to-peer electronic cash system that solved the longstanding double-spending problem that had hindered digital currencies' viability. By employing cryptographic signatures and a distributed ledger, Bitcoin ensured that each currency unit could only be spent once, maintaining scarcity and integrity.

The cryptographic techniques that support their security features are where cryptocurrency gets its given name. Transactions are safeguarded using public and private keys, a cryptographic has algorithms, and digital signatures, and users are given ownership and control over their digital assets. Public keys act as addresses to receive transactions, while private keys grant access and authorization to send funds from those addresses.

The revolutionary technology that powers cryptocurrencies is the blockchain. A blockchain is a transparent, tamper-proof digital ledger which stores every transaction made on a network of computers. After being verified, each block in the chain is connected to the one before it, creating an immutable chain of records. Each block in the chain comprises a series of transactions. This guarantees a transparent transaction history that everyone on the network can audit and verify.

The potential applications of cryptocurrencies extend far beyond simple peer-to-peer transactions. Blockchain technology also enables smart contracts, which are contracts that are self-executing with the conditions of the agreement built directly into the contract's code. These contracts eliminate the need for middlemen and offer a trustworthy means to conduct various business interactions when certain conditions are satisfied.

As the cryptocurrency ecosystem expanded, new cryptocurrencies, often called "altcoins," were introduced. These alternative cryptocurrencies sought to address limitations in Bitcoin and explore different use cases. Ethereum, for instance, introduced the concept of programmable smart contracts and decentralized applications (DApps), enabling developers to create a wide array of applications beyond simple currency transactions.

While the potential of cryptocurrencies is immense, it's important to note that the space has challenges. Regulatory uncertainties, security vulnerabilities, and price volatility are among the hurdles investors and cryptocurrency market participants must navigate. Nonetheless, the profound impact of cryptocurrencies on finance, technology, and even governance is undeniable.

In conclusion, cryptocurrencies represent a revolutionary departure from traditional financial systems. They harness the power of decentralized networks and cryptographic security to create digital assets that challenge conventional notions of money. Blockchain technology ensures transparency, immutability, and the potential for self-executing contracts. While the road ahead may be complex, cryptocurrencies continue to reshape industries and redefine how we think about value, transactions, and trust in the digital age.

How Cryptocurrencies Work: Blockchain Technology

At the heart of the cryptocurrency revolution lies an ingenious technological innovation: blockchain. This revolutionary technology is the foundation upon which cryptocurrencies operate, providing a transparent, secure, and decentralized framework for digital transactions and beyond. To truly grasp how cryptocurrencies work, one must delve into the intricacies of blockchain technology.

Imagine a digital ledger distributed across a network of computers, where transactions are recorded transparently and immutable. This is the essence of blockchain. A blockchain comprises a series of interconnected blocks, each containing a set of transactions. These blocks are cryptographically linked, forming a continuous chain resistant to tampering and alteration.

The security and integrity of a blockchain are established through cryptographic hashing. Each block contains a unique digital fingerprint, called a hash, generated using the information within the block and the previous block's hash. Any change in the data of a single block would require altering the data in all subsequent blocks, rendering the tampering evident and the chain broken. This characteristic guarantees the blockchain's immutability, making it a trusted and dependable source of data.

The decentralized nature of blockchain technology is one of its primary features. Traditional databases are typically centralized and controlled by a single entity that maintains and updates the records. In contrast, a blockchain is supported by a network of participants, often called nodes. Consensus mechanisms are used to verify and agree on the contents of each block, and each node maintains a copy of the whole blockchain. This decentralized consensus ensures that no single entity has complete control over the blockchain, enhancing security and eliminating the need for intermediaries.

The process of adding new transactions to a blockchain involves a consensus algorithm, with the most common being Proof of Work (PoW) and Proof of Stake (PoS). In proof-of-work (PoW), miners compete to solve challenging mathematical puzzles; the first to do so earns the right to add the next block and a reward. This process requires substantial computational power and energy consumption. PoS, on the other hand, relies on validators who lock up a certain amount of cryptocurrency as collateral. Intensive computations are reduced since validators are selected to build new blocks based on their stake.

Cryptocurrencies utilize blockchain technology to enable secure and transparent digital transactions. When a user initiates a cryptocurrency transaction, it is broadcast to the network. Miners or validators then group these transactions into a block and compete to solve the cryptographic puzzle associated with that block. Once solved, the block is added to the blockchain, and its transactions are confirmed and recorded permanently.

The decentralized nature of blockchain technology brings a level of trust to transactions that is unparalleled in traditional systems. In a centralized system, trust is vested in a single authority to validate transactions and maintain the integrity of records. However, this centralized control opens the door to manipulation, censorship, and single points of failure. In a blockchain, trust is distributed across the network, and consensus verifies transactions. This trustlessness eliminates the need to rely on intermediaries, reducing costs and increasing the efficiency of transactions.

Blockchain technology has applications far beyond cryptocurrencies. Its transparent, secure, and tamper-resistant nature makes it suitable for various industries and use cases. Smart contracts, for instance, are self-executing contracts with predefined rules written into code. These contracts automatically execute when conditions are met, eliminating the need for intermediaries in various business processes.

In conclusion, the intricate workings of cryptocurrencies are intimately tied to the revolutionary technology of blockchain. Blockchain's decentralized, transparent, and secure nature provides the backbone for cryptocurrencies, ensuring that transactions are recorded with integrity and trust. Beyond cryptocurrencies, blockchain's potential extends to reshaping industries, streamlining processes, and redefining the concept of trust in the digital age. As blockchain technology continues to evolve, it promises to transform not just how we transact digitally but how we interact with information and systems across various domains.

Key Terminologies Every Investor Should Know

Embarking on a journey into cryptocurrency investing requires more than just a sense of curiosity; it demands a solid understanding of the unique terminologies underpinning this dynamic landscape. From blockchain fundamentals to trading strategies, mastering the language of cryptocurrencies is essential for informed decision-making. Here, we explore key terminologies every investor should be familiar with, providing you with a foundational grasp of the language spoken in digital assets.

Blockchain:

The blockchain, a decentralized and immutable digital ledger, is at the core of cryptocurrencies. A blockchain consists of interconnected blocks, each containing a set of transactions. The blocks are cryptographically linked together, ensuring data integrity and transparency. The technology's application isn't confined to cryptocurrencies; it extends to various sectors seeking secure and tamper-resistant record-keeping.

Cryptocurrency:

Cryptocurrency is a term used to describe a form of virtual or digital money that uses cryptography to ensure the security of transactions. Bitcoin, the pioneer of cryptocurrencies, ignited this concept, and many altcoins (alternative cryptocurrencies) have since emerged. Each cryptocurrency operates on its blockchain, governing its rules and transactions.

Wallet:

A digital tool called a cryptocurrency wallet enables users to transmit, receive, and store cryptocurrencies. There are various kinds of wallets, including hardware wallets (physical objects), paper wallets (printed keys), and software wallets (online or mobile apps). Wallets are secured with private keys, which grant access to your digital assets.

Private Key and Public Key:

In the realm of cryptography, private keys and public keys are essential components. A private key is a secret code granting access to cryptocurrency holdings. It must be kept secure and never shared. A public key is derived from the private key and acts as an address for receiving funds. Sharing your public key is safe and necessary for receiving transactions.

Exchange:

Cryptocurrency exchanges are digital platforms where users can buy, sell, and trade cryptocurrencies. They come in various forms, from centralized exchanges (CEX) to decentralized exchanges (DEX). CEXs are operated by companies, while DEXs operate without a central authority, providing greater user control.

Altcoin:

Altcoins are any cryptocurrencies other than Bitcoin. They encompass various projects with varying purposes, from improving upon Bitcoin's limitations to offering innovative solutions in smart contracts, decentralized finance (DeFi), and more.

ICO, STO, IEO:

Initial Coin Offering (ICO), Security Token Offering (STO), and Initial Exchange Offering (IEO) are fundraising mechanisms for cryptocurrency projects. ICOs involve issuing tokens in exchange for investment, often for future use within a project. STOs involve tokens representing company ownership, much like traditional securities. IEOs are conducted through cryptocurrency exchanges, providing projects with a platform for fundraising.

FOMO and FUD:

These acronyms encapsulate two prevalent emotional drivers in the cryptocurrency market. FOMO also known as the Fear of Missing Out, refers to the anxiety that an investor might miss out on potential gains. FUD, or Fear, Uncertainty, and Doubt, involves spreading negative information to create doubt and panic in the market.

Hodl:

Originating from a typo of "hold," hodl has become a humorous term in the cryptocurrency community. It signifies the act of holding onto cryptocurrencies regardless of market fluctuations, indicating a long-term investment strategy.

Market Cap:

Market capitalization is the total value of a cryptocurrency in circulation. It's calculated by multiplying the cryptocurrency's current price by the total number of coins in circulation. Market cap provides an overview of a cryptocurrency's relative size in the market.

Bull and Bear Markets:

A bull market is known as a sustained period of rising prices and positive sentiment, while a bear market signifies a prolonged period of declining prices and pessimism. Understanding these cycles is crucial for assessing market trends and making informed decisions.

Tokenomics:

Tokenomics refers to the economic model and structure of a cryptocurrency or token. It encompasses factors such as supply, distribution, utility, and incentives within a project's ecosystem.

Decentralized Finance:

DeFi is a movement that aims to recreate traditional financial services using blockchain technology. It encompasses lending, borrowing, trading, and more, without relying on intermediaries like banks.

PoW (Proof of Work) and PoS (Proof of Stake): These

consensus mechanisms validate and add new transactions to a blockchain. PoW involves solving complex mathematical puzzles, while PoS relies on validators who lock up cryptocurrency as collateral.

Whales:

Whales are individuals or organizations that hold significant amounts of a particular cryptocurrency. Their large holdings can influence market dynamics, making the community closely watch their actions.

Satoshis:

Named after Bitcoin's creator, Satoshi Nakamoto, a satoshi is the smallest unit of Bitcoin. There are 100 million satoshis in one Bitcoin, allowing for precision in transactions and discussions about smaller amounts.
In conclusion, the landscape of cryptocurrency investing is rich with specialized terminologies that reflect the unique nature of digital assets. Understanding these terms is necessary for effective communication within the community and making informed investment decisions. As the cryptocurrency ecosystem evolves, mastering these key terminologies will be your compass in navigating this ever-changing realm.

Different Types of Cryptocurrencies

The world of cryptocurrencies is a diverse and rapidly evolving ecosystem, with many digital assets extending far beyond the pioneer, Bitcoin. These diverse digital currencies, often called cryptocurrencies or tokens, serve various purposes, from facilitating transactions to powering decentralized applications. Understanding the various types of cryptocurrencies is essential for investors and enthusiasts seeking to navigate this complex landscape. In this section, we delve into some of the most prominent categories of cryptocurrencies, each with its unique features, use cases, and innovations.

Bitcoin, the very first cryptocurrency, is both a digital currency and a store of value. Often referred to as "digital gold," Bitcoin's primary objective is to serve as a decentralized alternative to traditional fiat currencies. It boasts a capped supply of 21 million coins, ensuring scarcity and potentially safeguarding against inflation.

Bitcoin's primary use case is a hedge against economic uncertainty and a potential long-term investment.

Smart contract platforms go beyond simple currency transactions, enabling the creation of DApps (decentralized applications) and programmable digital contracts. Ethereum, the pioneering platform, introduced the concept of smart contracts, which are self-executing agreements with predefined rules. These contracts are coded onto the blockchain and automatically execute when conditions are met. Other platforms like Binance Smart Chain, Cardano, and Solana have entered the scene, offering improved scalability and features.

Privacy coins prioritize anonymity and confidentiality in transactions. They employ advanced cryptographic techniques to shield sender and receiver information and transaction amounts. Monero, for instance, uses ring signatures and stealth addresses to provide privacy. Zcash utilizes zero-knowledge proofs to verify transactions without revealing transaction details. Privacy coins cater to users seeking enhanced transaction privacy and fungibility.

Stablecoins are intended to keep their value stable, frequently pegged to a fiat currency like the US Dollar. They provide a bridge between the volatility of cryptocurrencies and the stability of traditional currencies. Tether (USDT), USD Coin (USDC), and DAI are prominent examples. Stablecoins are widely used for trading, transferring funds across borders, and as a base currency in decentralized exchanges.

Utility tokens are native to specific platforms and ecosystems, serving as a unit of value within those networks. They provide access to the platform's services, products, or features. Ethereum-based tokens, such as

Chainlink (LINK) and Uniswap (UNI), facilitate decentralized oracle services and decentralized exchanges, respectively. Utility tokens can represent ownership or participation rights within a project's ecosystem.

Security tokens represent ownership in real-world assets, such as real estate, company shares, or commodities. Security tokens are governed by regulatory standards and require compliance with securities laws, unlike utility tokens. Tokenizing real assets through security tokens offers increased liquidity, fractional ownership, and streamlined transferability.

Non-Fungible Tokens (NFTs) are unique digital assets representing ownership of particlar items, such as digital art, collectibles, virtual real estate, and tweets. NFTs are indivisible and cannot be exchanged on a one-to-one basis like cryptocurrencies. They utilize blockchain technology to verify authenticity and provenance, revolutionizing digital ownership and the concept of scarcity in the digital world.

Decentralized Finance (DeFi) tokens are integral to the rapidly growing DeFi ecosystem, which aims to recreate traditional financial services on blockchain platforms. DeFi tokens are often used for liquidity provision, yield farming, and governance within DeFi protocols. Tokens like AAVE, Compound (COMP), and Maker (MKR) empower users to lend, borrow, and earn interest on their assets without intermediaries.

Platform coins are native tokens associated with specific exchanges, services, or ecosystems. Binance Coin (BNB) and Huobi Token (HT) are examples of exchange-based platform coins. These tokens often provide trading fee discounts, access to premium features, and participation in platform governance.

Interoperability tokens aim to bridge different blockchain networks, enabling seamless communication and value transfer between disparate platforms. Polkadot (DOT) and Cosmos (ATOM) are examples of projects focusing on interoperability. They envision a future where various blockchains can collaborate and share resources.

In conclusion, cryptocurrencies are a diverse and multifaceted domain, encompassing a wide array of digital assets with distinct features and purposes. From digital gold like Bitcoin to the programmability of smart contract platforms and the uniqueness of NFTs, each type of cryptocurrency serves a particular role in reshaping finance, ownership, and interaction in the digital age. As the ecosystem evolves, understanding these various types of cryptocurrencies becomes crucial for making informed investment decisions and participating in innovative projects shaping our future.

CHAPTER II

Getting Started with Crypto Investments

Assessing Your Investment Goals and Risk Tolerance

Entering the world of cryptocurrency investment requires more than just a passing interest; it necessitates a thorough understanding of your personal investment goals and risk tolerance. The cryptocurrency market's dynamic and often volatile nature demands careful consideration and strategic planning to navigate its potential rewards and pitfalls. This section delves into the crucial process of determining your investment objectives and risk tolerance with regard to cryptocurrency investments, assisting you in reaching decisions that are in line with your goals and comfort level in terms of finance.

Investment goals serve as the guiding star in your cryptocurrency journey. Whether you aim to generate substantial returns, diversify your portfolio, or explore the technology's potential, clarifying your investment goals is paramount. Are you seeking short-term gains through active trading, or are you in it for the long haul, aiming to capitalize on the potential of a particular blockchain project? It is essential to specify your investing horizon, whether short-, medium-, or long-term, to customize your approach and make it compatible with your goals.

Assessing your risk tolerance is a cornerstone of any investment endeavor, and the volatile nature of the cryptocurrency market makes this evaluation particularly pertinent. Your capacity and willingness to deal with changes in the value of your investments are referred to as your risk tolerance. When establishing your risk tolerance, take into account your financial circumstances, investment experience, and emotional fortitude. Do you feel at ease with the possibility of major price swings, or does the thought of temporary losses give you nightmares? Being honest about your risk appetite will guide your investment decisions and help you avoid making impulsive choices driven by market sentiment.

Cryptocurrency investments offer a compelling mix of risk and reward, and striking the right balance is essential. Higher potential returns often correlate with higher risk levels. A low-risk approach might involve investing in established, well-known cryptocurrencies like Bitcoin and Ethereum, while a higher-risk strategy could involve exploring emerging altcoins with the potential for substantial gains. As you assess your investment goals and risk tolerance, consider your investment horizon and the proportion of your portfolio you're comfortable allocating to cryptocurrency.

The age-old adage "Don't put all your eggs in one basket" holds true in the world of cryptocurrency investments. Spreading your investments over many assets is known as diversification, and it is a method used to lessen the negative effects of a single asset's underperformance on your portfolio as a whole. Investing in a variety of known cryptocurrencies, promising altcoins, as well as DeFi projects is one way to diversify one's holdings in the cryptocurrency market. However, diversification should be approached with caution; over-diversification can dilute potential gains and create a portfolio that's difficult to manage.

Mitigating risks in the cryptocurrency market begins with thorough research and due diligence. Understand the projects you're investing in, their use cases, development teams, and roadmaps. Scrutinize whitepapers, project updates, and community sentiment. Consider the technology's potential for adoption and the unique challenges it may face. While risk can never be entirely eliminated, a well-informed investor can make more educated decisions and minimize the impact of unexpected events.

The cryptocurrency market is notorious for its volatility, leading to emotional highs and lows. Fear of missing out (FOMO) during rapid price rallies and succumbing to panic during market dips can result in impulsive decisions. It is crucial to develop a rational and disciplined approach to investing. Setting clear entry and exit points, establishing stop-loss orders, and sticking to your investment plan can help you navigate the emotional roller coaster and make decisions grounded in logic rather than emotions.

The cryptocurrency landscape is constantly evolving, and staying informed is crucial. Engage in ongoing education through reputable sources, forums, and communities. Keep up with technological advancements, regulatory changes, and market trends. The more you understand about the market, the better equipped you'll be to adapt your investment strategy as needed.

In conclusion, assessing your investment goals and risk tolerance is a fundamental step in your cryptocurrency investment journey. It serves as the foundation upon which you'll build your strategy, allocate your resources, and make informed decisions. By understanding your objectives, acknowledging your risk comfort zone, and conducting diligent research, you can tailor your cryptocurrency investments to align with your aspirations while managing potential risks. Although the cryptocurrency industry is not for the faint of heart, you may manage its complexity and take advantage of its prospects with careful planning and a logical approach.

Creating a Cryptocurrency Investment Strategy

A well-thought-out investment strategy that fits your goals, risk tolerance, and market knowledge is needed when investing in cryptocurrencies. It goes beyond simple speculating. The cryptocurrency market's dynamic and ever-changing nature calls for a deliberate strategy that goes beyond following trends and hype. In this section, we delve into the crucial components of crafting a cryptocurrency investment strategy, guiding you through building a solid foundation for successful and informed investment decisions.

Before diving into the cryptocurrency market, define clear and achievable investment goals. Are you seeking short-term gains through active trading or aiming for long-term growth and stability? Your goals will influence the time horizon of your investments and the strategies you employ. Whether it's capital appreciation, portfolio diversification, or participation in specific blockchain projects, having a well-defined purpose will serve as your compass throughout your investment journey.

Risk tolerance is a critical factor in shaping your investment strategy. Evaluate your emotional capacity to endure market volatility and potential losses. Are you a risk-averse investor seeking stable growth, or are you comfortable with higher risk for the chance of substantial returns? Your level of risk tolerance will affect the kinds of cryptocurrencies you look at, how much funds you invest, and when you decide to make an investment.

Cryptocurrency investments can span various timeframes, each with its own set of strategies. Short-term traders capitalize on price volatility, often employing technical analysis and short-lived trends. Medium-term investors might focus on promising projects with development milestones on the horizon. Long-term investors, often referred to as "HODLers," hold cryptocurrencies for extended periods, believing in their potential value over time. Your investment horizon should align with your goals and risk tolerance.

Any investing strategy, even one including cryptocurrency, should adhere to the fundamental principle of diversification. Make sure to diversify your holdings over a variety of cryptocurrencies, including well-known ones like Bitcoin and Ethereum, as well as promising altcoins and potentially decentralized finance (DeFi) tokens. Through diversification, you can lessen the effect of a single asset's underperformance on your entire portfolio. However, avoid over-diversification, which can dilute potential gains.

Informed decisions are the cornerstone of successful cryptocurrency investments. Thoroughly research the projects you're considering, assessing their whitepapers, development teams, use cases, and market potential. Engage with reputable communities and sources of information. Understand the technological nuances, regulatory landscape, and competitive positioning of the cryptocurrencies you're interested in. Due diligence minimizes the risks associated with misinformation and scam projects.

In order to forecast future price changes, technical analysis examines price charts, patterns, as well as indicators. Fundamental analysis delves into the underlying factors that drive a cryptocurrency's value, such as technology, adoption, and market trends. A balanced approach to both analyses can provide a comprehensive perspective, guiding your entry and exit points.

Setting clear entry and exit points is essential for disciplined investing. Decide the price range at which you'll enter a trade or make an investment and the criteria to trigger an exit. Implementing stop-loss orders and take-profit targets can protect your capital from sudden market fluctuations and help you avoid making emotionally-driven decisions.

Risk management is a cornerstone of any investment strategy. Never make an investment you cannot afford to lose. Consider limiting your exposure to a single cryptocurrency to a certain percentage of your portfolio. Determine how much you're willing to risk on a trade or investment and adhere to these limits.

The cryptocurrency market is dynamic, with news, technological advancements, and regulatory changes influencing prices and trends. Stay informed through reputable news sources, forums, and social media. Be ready to adapt your strategy as the market evolves while resisting the urge to make impulsive decisions based on short-term market sentiment.

Successful cryptocurrency investing requires patience and discipline. Markets can experience extreme volatility, but succumbing to emotions can lead to impulsive decisions. Stick to your strategy, avoid chasing quick gains, and remember that the cryptocurrency market operates 24/7, allowing for measured decisions rather than rushed actions.

In conclusion, crafting a cryptocurrency investment strategy systematically involves defining your goals, assessing your risk tolerance, and aligning your approach with your investment horizon. By diversifying your portfolio, conducting thorough research, and employing technical and fundamental analysis, you can make informed decisions that mitigate risks and capitalize on opportunities. Staying updated, remaining disciplined, and adapting to market dynamics will contribute to a resilient and adaptable investment strategy that can weather the complexities of the cryptocurrency landscape.

Choosing the Right Exchange Platform

In the world of cryptocurrency investing, the choice of a suitable exchange platform can significantly impact your trading experience and investment outcomes. Cryptocurrency exchanges serve as gateways to the digital asset realm, facilitating the buying, selling, and trading of various cryptocurrencies. As the market continues to expand, the options for exchange platforms have grown in both number and diversity. However, not all exchanges are made equal, so choosing the best platform demands giving serious thought to aspects that match your requirements, preferences, and investing objectives. In this section, we delve into the critical aspects of choosing the right cryptocurrency exchange platform, empowering you to make informed decisions that optimize your trading journey.

Security is paramount in cryptocurrency, where hacks and breaches have made headlines. Prioritize exchange platforms with a proven track record of security measures along with a reputation for protecting users' assets when evaluating them. Research the platform's history of security incidents, review user feedback, and assess whether it employs industry-standard security practices such as two-factor authentication (2FA), cold storage for funds, and regular security audits.

Regulatory compliance is a critical consideration when choosing an exchange platform. Opt for platforms that operate within the legal frameworks of your jurisdiction and adhere to anti-money laundering (AML) and know-your-customer (KYC) regulations. An exchange's commitment to regulatory compliance speaks to its commitment to transparency and legitimacy.

Different exchange platforms offer varying selections of cryptocurrencies for trading. If you're interested in specific altcoins beyond Bitcoin and Ethereum, ensure that the exchange you choose supports the cryptocurrencies you wish to trade. Additionally, assess the quality of the projects listed on the exchange; avoiding platforms that list suspicious or low-quality tokens can mitigate risk.

A user-friendly interface can significantly enhance your trading experience. Look for an exchange with an intuitive interface, responsive design, and clear navigation. A clutter-free and well-organized platform can streamline your trading activities and reduce the likelihood of errors during transactions.

The simplicity of buying or selling an asset without creating major price changes is known as liquidity. High liquidity ensures you can execute trades swiftly and at a fair price. Research the exchange's trading volumes and order book depth for the cryptocurrencies you're interested in to ensure sufficient liquidity.

Different exchange platforms charge varying fees for trading, deposits, and withdrawals. Compare fee structures and assess whether they align with your trading frequency and volume. While low fees can be attractive, remember that quality of service and security should not be compromised solely for cost savings.

Customer support is crucial, especially in technical glitches or account-related issues. Research the quality and responsiveness of the exchange's customer support team. Search for platforms that provide a variety of support options, such as email, live chat, and social media, and make sure that their response times meet your standards.

Be mindful about the exchange's deposit and withdrawal options. Some platforms support direct bank transfers, credit cards, and various cryptocurrencies, while others may have limited options. Choose an exchange that provides convenient and secure methods for funding and withdrawing your account.

A mobile app can provide flexibility for trading on the go. If you prefer trading from your mobile device, consider exchanges that offer well-designed and secure mobile apps. Ensure that the app provides essential features like real-time price tracking, order placement, and account management.

Some exchanges offer educational resources, market analysis, and trading tools to support users' knowledge and decision-making. To aid you in making knowledgeable trading selections and staying current on market trends, take into account platforms that offer instructional content, tips, and insights.

Geographic restrictions can affect your ability to access and trade on specific exchange platforms. Ensure the platform is available and accessible in your region to avoid any limitations or complications related to account creation and usage.

Beyond official reviews and ratings, tap into the cryptocurrency community's feedback on various platforms. Online forums, social media groups, and cryptocurrency communities often provide valuable insights into the experiences of other traders. This can help you gain a well-rounded perspective on the strengths and weaknesses of different exchange platforms.

In conclusion, choosing the right cryptocurrency exchange platform is critical in your trading journey. Evaluating factors such as security, reputation, range of cryptocurrencies, user interface, liquidity, trading fees, customer support, deposit and withdrawal methods, mobile app availability, education, and geographic restrictions will guide your decision-making process. A thorough assessment of these factors ensures that the platform you choose aligns with your trading preferences, investment goals, and risk tolerance, setting the stage for a successful and rewarding trading experience in the vibrant world of cryptocurrencies.

Setting Up Your Wallet: Hot vs. Cold Wallets

Securing your cryptocurrency holdings is of paramount importance in the ever-evolving digital landscape. As the popularity of cryptocurrencies continues to rise, so does the need for robust wallet solutions to safeguard your digital assets. An important option that can considerably affect the security of your holdings is whether to use a hot wallet or a cold wallet. Each type of wallet has advantages and trade-offs, catering to different levels of convenience, accessibility, and protection. In this section, we delve into the intricacies of hot and cold wallets, providing a comprehensive understanding to make an informed choice that aligns with your security needs and usage preferences.

Hot or online wallets are digital wallets connected to the internet. They offer high convenience and accessibility, making them suitable for frequent transactions, online purchases, and day-to-day use. Hot wallets include various forms, such as software wallets (desktop, mobile, or web-based) and exchange wallets. While hot wallets provide instant access to your funds, they also come with higher security risks due to their online connectivity.

Convenience is a notable advantage of hot wallets. They are user-friendly and easy to set up, allowing quick access to your funds and enabling swift transactions. Additionally, hot wallets provide accessibility from anywhere with an internet connection, making them valuable for active traders and users who engage in frequent transactions. The sending and receiving of cryptocurrencies is made simple by the many hot wallets' user-friendly interfaces.

However, hot wallets also come with security considerations. Being connected to the internet exposes them to online threats such as hacking, phishing attacks, and malware. Compromised devices could potentially lead to the loss of your funds. Exchange wallets, a type of hot wallet, are subject to the security measures of the exchange platform. If the exchange is breached, your funds might be compromised. Regular updates are necessary to mitigate vulnerabilities in hot wallet software, as neglecting updates can expose your wallet to known security risks.

On the other hand, cold wallets, also known as offline wallets, are designed to keep your private keys and cryptocurrencies entirely offline. They provide unparalleled security, making them suitable for storing significant amounts of cryptocurrencies for the long term. Cold wallets include hardware and paper wallets, each offering unique features that minimize the risks associated with online exposure.

Cold wallets prioritize security and are considered the most secure cryptocurrency storage option. Their offline nature makes them immune to online threats like hacking and malware. Cold wallets also reduce the risk of unauthorized access or exposure by storing private keys offline. These wallets are ideal for the long-term storage of cryptocurrencies that you don't plan to access frequently, protecting your holdings from day-to-day online risks.

However, cold wallets also come with considerations. They are less accessible than hot wallets, as accessing funds from a cold wallet requires transferring assets to a hot wallet first. Cold wallets like hardware wallets are physical devices that can be lost, stolen, or damaged. Therefore, keeping them in a secure location is crucial. Additionally, there might be a learning curve associated with setting up and using hardware wallets, particularly for individuals new to the cryptocurrency space.

Choosing the Right Wallet Solution is a decision that requires a careful balance between security needs and usage patterns. A hot wallet might be preferred for users who frequently transact and value convenience. However, those prioritizing the long-term storage and protection of substantial holdings would find a cold wallet the superior choice due to its unmatched security.

Some cryptocurrency enthusiasts opt for a Hybrid Solution, which combines the advantages of both hot and cold wallets. This approach involves using a hot wallet for day-to-day transactions and a cold wallet for securely storing larger amounts of cryptocurrencies. The hybrid approach allows for frequent access to funds while ensuring that most holdings remain secure offline.

Adhering to Security Best Practices is essential regardless of the chosen wallet type. Regularly backing up wallet information, using strong passwords, enabling two-factor authentication (2FA), avoiding phishing attempts, and keeping software updated are universally applicable principles that enhance the security of your digital assets.

In conclusion, whether you opt for the convenience of a hot wallet or the security of a cold wallet, your choice should align with your security requirements, usage patterns, and the value of your cryptocurrency holdings. Hot wallets provide accessibility and ease of use, making them suitable for frequent transactions. Cold wallets prioritize security by keeping private keys offline and protecting your holdings from online threats. Regardless of your choice, robust security practices are crucial for safeguarding your digital assets in the dynamic world of cryptocurrencies.

CHAPTER III

Fundamental Analysis for Crypto Investments

Evaluating Whitepapers and Project Concepts

In the dynamic realm of cryptocurrency investments, evaluating whitepapers and project concepts takes center stage as a critical determinant of success. With the proliferation of blockchain projects offering diverse solutions, the ability to discern viable ventures from speculative endeavors is paramount. The whitepaper, often the cornerstone of a project's introduction, is a comprehensive document outlining the project's vision, technology, use cases, and implementation strategies. Delving into the world of whitepapers and project concepts is an intellectual endeavor that demands a multifaceted assessment to make informed investment decisions. In this section, we delve into the intricacies of evaluating whitepapers and project concepts, providing you with a comprehensive guide to navigate the landscape of cryptocurrency investments.

At the heart of the evaluation process lies the whitepaper, a document designed to elucidate the intricate details of a cryptocurrency project. Authored by the project's developers or team, a whitepaper serves as a testament to the project's vision, outlining its objectives, underlying technology, real-world applications, and roadmap for development. A diligent whitepaper review is essential, moving beyond superficial overviews to grasp the technical foundations, innovative propositions, and tangible contributions the project aims to deliver.

An integral aspect of assessing any cryptocurrency project is understanding the team responsible for its realization. The team's expertise, credibility, and collective experience can greatly influence the project's execution and ultimate success. Scrutinize the profiles of team members, explore their past involvements in the blockchain space, and assess their contributions to the broader cryptocurrency ecosystem. A competent team with a broad range of skills and a history of relevant successes strengthens investor confidence and increases the project's validity.

At the core of any promising cryptocurrency project is the capacity to address a genuine problem with an innovative solution. As you assess project concepts, delve into the authenticity of the problem being tackled. Does it resonate with current market needs, and is the proposed solution both practical and innovative? Scrutinize how the project leverages blockchain technology to deliver distinct advantages and evaluate its comprehension of the industry it aims to revolutionize or enhance.

The technological framework underlying a cryptocurrency project is a linchpin of its viability. In the world of whitepapers, deciphering the technical intricacies is essential. Does the project introduce groundbreaking advancements such as consensus mechanisms, scalability solutions, or privacy enhancements? A comprehensive grasp of the technical feasibility, security measures, and potential for adopting the proposed technology is imperative to gauge the project's potential.

A cryptocurrency project's utility hinges on its real-world applications. Probe the whitepaper for use cases that transcend hypothetical scenarios. Does the project's scope align with the current market landscape, addressing niche requirements or offering innovative solutions? Assess the potential market size and demand for the project's use cases. Projects with diverse applications that can drive widespread adoption are often more appealing to potential investors.

Tokenomics, the economic model underlying a project's native token, is another facet of evaluation. The token's role within the ecosystem, distribution mechanisms, and strategies to maintain scarcity and value are critical factors to consider. An intelligently designed tokenomics model should incentivize participation, contribute to network security, and ensure the project's sustainability over the long term.

Understanding the competitive landscape is pivotal. Examine the project's positioning vis-à-vis existing players in the market. What sets the project apart? Evaluate its competitive advantages, differentiation factors, and potential challenges in gaining market share. A project that effectively addresses a market gap or offers unique value propositions is better poised for success. The

roadmap embedded within the whitepaper offers insights into a project's developmental trajectory. Is the roadmap coherent, with tangible milestones that are both transparent and achievable? Clear communication about development progress and regular updates speak to the project's accountability. Investigate the progress achieved since the whitepaper's publication, looking for tangible evidence of advancements made.

Community engagement and adoption rates provide valuable insights into a project's vitality. Scrutinize the project's online presence, social media interactions, and community engagement levels. An engaged community can contribute to awareness, adoption, and network growth. The project's collaborations, partnerships, or endorsements from reputable entities also indicate its potential for success.

Compliance is essential for a project's sustainability in a rapidly evolving regulatory landscape. Analyze how well the project adheres with compliance requirements and addresses legal problems. A project demonstrating a proactive approach to regulatory considerations will likely thrive in a regulated environment.

Evaluating whitepapers and project concepts is a nuanced process that demands critical thinking and meticulous due diligence. Engage in comprehensive research, scrutinize all available information, seek expert input, and participate in discussions within the cryptocurrency community. Beware of projects that overpromise returns, need more transparency, or rely solely on hype.

In conclusion, evaluating whitepapers and project concepts is a cornerstone of informed cryptocurrency investment. By dissecting the whitepaper's content, assessing the team's credibility, understanding the project's real-world applicability, analyzing technology and innovation, scrutinizing tokenomics, considering market potential, evaluating the competitive landscape, exploring the roadmap, gauging community engagement, and acknowledging regulatory considerations, you can navigate the complexities of the cryptocurrency realm with greater acumen. Your capacity to distinguish between visionary projects and speculative ventures will be crucial in determining the success of your cryptocurrency investments as the landscape evolves.

Understanding Market Capitalization, Supply, and Circulation

Understanding key metrics is paramount to informed decision-making in the captivating world of cryptocurrency investments. Among these metrics, market capitalization, supply, and circulation are fundamental indicators that provide insights into a cryptocurrency's value, potential, and dynamics. A thorough understanding of these measures is necessary for navigating the complexity of cryptocurrency investing as the market continues to develop and diversify. In this section, we delve into the intricacies of market capitalization, supply, and circulation, unraveling their significance and unveiling the nuanced insights they offer to astute investors.

A popular metric for measuring a cryptocurrency's overall value is market capitalization. Calculated by multiplying the current or present price of a single cryptocurrency unit by its total circulating supply, market capitalization is often presented as a measure of a cryptocurrency's relative size within the broader market. While it serves as a quick reference for comparison, it is essential to recognize its limitations and delve deeper into its implications.

Market capitalization offers a snapshot of the total value locked in a cryptocurrency, indicating its relative position in the market hierarchy. However, it can be misleading when viewed in isolation. Cryptocurrencies with larger market capitalizations are not inherently superior; rather, market dynamics, adoption rates, and project fundamentals significantly influence their trajectories. Newer projects with innovative technology and use cases might have lower market capitalizations, yet possess significant growth potential.

Supply and circulation metrics provide insights into the availability and movement of a cryptocurrency within the market. Supply refers to the total number of coins that will ever exist, which is predetermined by the cryptocurrency's protocol. Circulation, on the other hand, refers to the number of coins actively traded and available in the market.

Understanding supply and circulation is crucial for assessing scarcity and potential future price movements. Cryptocurrencies with limited supply, such as Bitcoin with its capped supply of 21 million coins, might experience price appreciation due to scarcity-driven demand. Conversely, projects with large supplies may face challenges in maintaining value if not accompanied by robust use cases and demand.

Token distribution and ownership shed light on the decentralization and concentration of wealth within a cryptocurrency ecosystem. Analyzing the distribution of coins across addresses can reveal the level of decentralization and whether a few entities hold a disproportionately large share of the supply. Projects with more evenly distributed tokens tend to align with the ethos of decentralization and community participation.

On the other hand, concentration of ownership can introduce the potential for market manipulation. Whales—entities holding significant amounts of a cryptocurrency—can influence market movements through large transactions. Monitoring token distribution can provide insights into the level of potential market manipulation and the degree of decentralization.

Circulating supply influences a cryptocurrency's price and overall market performance. Cryptocurrencies with lower circulating supplies might experience more volatile price movements due to lower liquidity. Significant price changes can be caused by a relatively small purchase or sell order. In contrast, cryptocurrencies with larger circulating supplies often exhibit greater price stability.

Inflation, the rate at which new coins are added to the circulating supply, also impacts a cryptocurrency's value. Projects with high inflation rates might struggle to maintain value over time, as newly minted coins can dilute existing holdings. Evaluating a cryptocurrency's inflation rate is crucial for assessing its long-term viability and potential for value preservation.

Ultimately, the value of a cryptocurrency is closely tied to its real-world utility and demand. A cryptocurrency with a compelling use case and widespread adoption is more likely to experience sustained value appreciation. Assessing the practical applications of a cryptocurrency within industries, sectors, or decentralized networks is essential for gauging its long-term potential.

Projects that generate genuine demand for their tokens by providing essential services, facilitating transactions, or solving real-world problems are better positioned to weather market volatility. Demand-driven value proposition and a strong user base are key indicators of a cryptocurrency's resilience and long-term growth potential.

Market sentiment and external factors significantly influence the metrics of market capitalization, supply, and circulation. Positive news, partnerships, technological advancements, and regulatory developments can drive up demand and consequently impact market capitalization. Conversely, negative news or regulatory hurdles can lead to rapid value erosion.

Investors must stay attuned to market sentiment and the broader macroeconomic landscape, as these factors can introduce volatility and uncertainty. While these external dynamics are beyond the control of individual investors, staying informed and adaptable is essential for managing risks and seizing opportunities.

In conclusion, a comprehensive understanding of market capitalization, supply, and circulation is imperative for navigating the intricate landscape of cryptocurrency investments. These metrics offer nuanced insights into a cryptocurrency's value, scarcity, demand, and growth potential. While market capitalization provides a broad measure of size, supply and circulation shed light on scarcity and liquidity. Examining token distribution and ownership reveals the level of decentralization and potential for market manipulation. Evaluating the influence of circulating supply and inflation on value is crucial, as is recognizing the impact of use cases and demand. Furthermore, market sentiment and external factors introduce catalysts and risks that shape the dynamic cryptocurrency ecosystem. Armed with this nuanced comprehension, investors can make informed decisions, positioning themselves for success in the captivating world of cryptocurrency investments.

Analyzing the Development Team and Roadmap

In cryptocurrency investments' dynamic and intricate world, an investor's ability to make informed decisions rests on a foundation of meticulous analysis. Two paramount factors that demand profound scrutiny are the development team behind a cryptocurrency project and the roadmap that outlines its future trajectory. These elements serve as guiding stars, illuminating the path toward potential investments in a landscape characterized by innovation and uncertainty. In this section, we delve into the nuanced process of meticulously analyzing the development team and roadmap, uncovering their immense significance and revealing the invaluable insights they offer to judicious investors.

At the heart of any successful cryptocurrency project lies the development team's collective vision, expertise, and dedication. This ensemble of innovators, technologists, and thought leaders is the driving force that conceives, architects, and actualizes the project's mission. A comprehensive analysis of the development team entails delving into their individual backgrounds, skill sets, and track records. These individuals are the architects of innovation, and their proficiency in blockchain technology, software development, cryptography, and related domains profoundly influences the project's feasibility and technical execution.

Furthermore, the composition of the development team plays a pivotal role. A diverse group of individuals, each with a unique skill set, indicates a well-rounded team capable of addressing multifaceted challenges. The presence of experts with a history of successful contributions to the blockchain community bolsters the project's credibility. Conversely, a team lacking relevant experience or members associated with unsuccessful or contentious projects raises valid concerns about the project's overall legitimacy.

Transparency is a hallmark of a reputable development team. Their commitment to open communication, community engagement, and accountability is often reflected in their online presence, responsiveness to queries, and willingness to address concerns. A team that actively interacts with the community fosters trust and showcases their dedication to the project's long-term success.

Complementing the development team is the project's roadmap—a meticulously laid-out strategic plan that charts the course of the project's evolution. The roadmap serves as a tangible manifestation of the project's ambitions, outlining the key milestones, technological advancements, and anticipated achievements. An adept roadmap analysis provides investors with insights into the project's overarching vision and practical implementation.

A well-structured roadmap is more than just a chronological sequence of events; it is a comprehensive narrative that concisely communicates the project's trajectory. It should offer a clear delineation of major milestones, such as mainnet launches, protocol upgrades, partnerships, and adoption targets. A roadmap that balances ambitious aspirations with pragmatic timelines demonstrates the project's level-headed approach and its capacity to navigate the complexities of execution.

However, a prudent investor should remain cautious of overly optimistic roadmaps that promise rapid and aggressive development. Unrealistic timelines can be indicative of a lack of understanding of the intricacies and challenges associated with blockchain development. A well-calibrated roadmap strikes a harmonious equilibrium between aspirational objectives and a realistic acknowledgment of the complexities involved.

A comprehensive approach is paramount when embarking on the journey of analyzing the development team and roadmap. Several crucial criteria form the bedrock of a judicious evaluation. Expertise and experience are pivotal factors—scrutinize team members' backgrounds and skill sets to ensure they possess the knowledge necessary to translate the project's vision into a tangible reality. Transparency and communication are equally crucial, reflecting the team's accountability and willingness to engage with the community.

The achievability of the roadmap's milestones and the practicality of its timelines also merit close examination. A roadmap should serve as a roadmap to attainable achievements, not a hasty sprint to meet unrealistic deadlines. The alignment of the roadmap with the project's overarching vision is indicative of a thoughtful and strategic approach. Adaptability and flexibility, especially in the context of the dynamic cryptocurrency landscape, signify a team's capacity to navigate unexpected challenges and seize opportunities. Partnerships and collaborations underscore a project's reach, credibility, and potential for growth.

The depth of community engagement provides a glimpse into the level of support and enthusiasm surrounding a project. Vibrant discussions and active feedback channels are indicative of a community that is deeply invested in the project's success. Understanding the development team's past achievements and learning experiences offers insights into their adaptability and commitment to continual improvement. Lastly, recognizing the influence of market sentiment and external factors on a project's trajectory is essential to maintaining a holistic perspective.

In the intricate tapestry of cryptocurrency investments, a judicious analysis of the development team and roadmap emerges as an indispensable endeavor. A project's development team embodies the architects of innovation, and their expertise, dedication, and adaptability significantly influence the project's prospects. Conversely, the roadmap functions as a compass, guiding the project's growth and execution. By meticulously evaluating the development team's expertise, transparency, and experience, and carefully scrutinizing the practicality and alignment of the roadmap, investors can position themselves for success in the ever-evolving cryptocurrency landscape. In a realm marked by both opportunity and risk, the ability to discern visionary projects from speculative ventures rests on a comprehensive understanding of these pivotal components.

Exploring Use Cases and Adoption Potential

Within the dynamic realm of cryptocurrency investments, the exploration of use cases and adoption potential stands as a pivotal venture for informed decision-making. Cryptocurrencies, rooted in blockchain technology, have transcended their initial role as mere alternatives to traditional financial systems. They have evolved into versatile instruments with a multitude of practical applications across various industries. Understanding these applications and the potential for widespread adoption is essential for investors seeking to navigate the intricate landscape of crypto investments.

At the core of cryptocurrencies' rise is their diverse use cases extending well beyond monetary transactions. While their origins can be traced to facilitating peer-to-peer financial exchanges, their potential applications now encompass realms such as supply chain management, healthcare, identity verification, and even the gaming industry. For instance, Bitcoin and Litecoin have become popular as hedges against economic uncertainty and means of sending money across borders, in addition to continuing to be used as stores of value and mediums of exchange. These digital assets offer a decentralized and censorship-resistant alternative to traditional financial systems.

The introduction of smart contracts, most notably by Ethereum, has revolutionized sectors that rely heavily on contractual agreements. These self-executing contracts eliminate intermediaries and streamline processes through automation, ensuring trustless execution. They have found applications in real estate transactions, supply chain logistics, and the rapidly expanding decentralized finance (DeFi) space, where transparency and tamper-proof execution are paramount.

Furthermore, the emergence of tokens on blockchain platforms has introduced a novel paradigm for ownership and representation of real-world assets. Security tokens, for instance, have enabled the digitization of ownership in assets such as real estate, art, and commodities. This innovation not only provides fractional ownership and enhanced liquidity but also diminishes traditional barriers to entry for a broader range of investors.

The potential for adoption of cryptocurrencies and blockchain technology extends well beyond their technical capabilities. Mass adoption rests at the crossroads of technological feasibility, practical usability, regulatory alignment, and societal acceptance. Cryptocurrencies are poised to address several global challenges, and their adoption has the potential to drive transformative changes across various sectors.

Financial inclusion is a significant facet of adoption potential. Cryptocurrencies promise to provide access to financial services for the billions of unbanked and underbanked individuals globally. Through the simplicity of smartphone access, individuals can become participants in the global economy, access essential financial services, and securely store value, even in regions with limited banking infrastructure.

Decentralized Finance (DeFi), a rapidly expanding sector within the blockchain space, is reshaping traditional financial systems. DeFi equips individuals with a variety of financial tools and services by providing services including loan, borrowing, trading, and yield farming without the use of middlemen. This open and permissionless ecosystem ensures inclusivity, enabling individuals from all walks of life to engage with sophisticated financial products and services.

Supply chain management, a traditionally complex and opaque process, is being revolutionized by blockchain technology. Through its inherent transparency and traceability, blockchain enhances accountability and safeguards ethical sourcing across industries such as agriculture, pharmaceuticals, and luxury goods. This technology addresses growing consumer demand for transparent and sustainable supply chains.

Healthcare and identity verification are other domains with immense blockchain adoption potential. The secure and interoperable nature of patient records stored on a blockchain could streamline healthcare processes and protect sensitive medical data. Blockchain-based identity systems promise to provide secure and portable identities, a solution particularly relevant for refugees and individuals without formal identification.

Non-fungible tokens (NFTs) have transformed the landscape in gaming and virtual assets. NFTs enable ownership and trade of unique in-game items, virtual real estate, digital art, collectibles, and even tokenized real-world assets. This innovation has profound implications for creators, collectors, and the broader gaming industry, creating new revenue streams and fostering engagement.

While the potential for adoption is promising, cryptocurrencies also face several barriers. Regulatory uncertainty poses challenges for both project development and investor confidence. Varying regulatory approaches across jurisdictions can impact the adoption of cryptocurrencies, creating an environment of uncertainty that must be navigated. Clear and supportive regulations can foster innovation and investment, while a lack thereof might impede progress.

Scalability remains a pressing concern for public blockchains. As adoption grows, the network's capacity to handle increasing transactions becomes critical. Solutions such as layer-2 protocols and sharding aim to address these challenges and enhance scalability without compromising security.

Education and usability are also significant barriers to adoption. The complex nature of blockchain technology and technical jargon can deter mainstream users from engaging with cryptocurrencies. Overcoming these barriers requires the development of user-friendly interfaces, educational initiatives, and a seamless integration of blockchain solutions into everyday life.

Concerns about security have also influenced adoption. High-profile hacks and vulnerabilities have highlighted the risks associated with cryptocurrencies. While blockchain technology inherently provides robust security mechanisms, ongoing development of advanced security measures is essential to instill confidence in both users and investors.

Environmental impact is another consideration, especially in the context of energy consumption associated with certain consensus mechanisms. Proof-of-Work (PoW), the consensus mechanism employed by Bitcoin, has raised concerns due to its energy-intensive nature. Transitioning to more environmentally friendly consensus mechanisms, such as Proof-of-Stake (PoS), represents a priority for both sustainability and adoption potential.

In the realm of cryptocurrency investments, understanding the diverse use cases and the potential for adoption holds significant implications. Investment opportunities are intrinsically linked to projects that address real-world challenges, demonstrate tangible value, and exhibit a clear path to adoption. An astute investor considers several critical factors when assessing potential investments.

Technological innovation plays a pivotal role. Projects that leverage cutting-edge technology to address existing inefficiencies hold significant promise for adoption. It is paramount to assess how the technology aligns with the project's use case and its potential to disrupt traditional systems.

Market demand is another crucial aspect. Investigating the current market landscape and identifying areas where blockchain solutions could bring substantial improvements is essential. Projects that cater to existing demand are more likely to gain traction and achieve meaningful adoption.

Regulatory compliance must be addressed. A project's alignment with regulatory frameworks is vital for long-term success. Regulatory compliance fosters stability and reduces the risks associated with legal uncertainties, enabling projects to flourish in a well-defined legal framework.

Partnerships and collaborations are pivotal for projects aiming to achieve widespread adoption. Collaborations with established enterprises and institutions can accelerate adoption by providing resources, credibility, and access to existing user bases. Partnerships enhance a project's potential for growth and amplify its impact.

Community engagement is a telling sign of a project's potential for success. Vibrant and active communities demonstrate enthusiasm and support, showcasing the project's ability to foster a dedicated user base that is instrumental in driving adoption.

Scalability solutions are critical for projects that aspire to handle increased adoption without compromising performance. Innovations addressing scalability concerns, such as layer-2 solutions and sharding, position projects to accommodate growing user bases while maintaining efficient network operation.

In conclusion, the exploration of use cases and adoption potential within the cryptocurrency landscape unveils a journey that intersects technology, innovation, economics, and societal transformation. Cryptocurrencies are no longer mere theoretical constructs; they are practical tools poised to reshape industries, empower individuals, and drive financial inclusion. The potential for adoption lies at the confluence of technological prowess, regulatory support, market demand, and societal readiness. The discerning investor recognizes that successful projects extend beyond speculative investments; they are solutions primed to address real-world challenges. Through comprehensive assessments of practical utility, technological innovation, regulatory landscapes, and market demand, investors can confidently traverse the landscape, identifying opportunities that align with their investment goals. As the cryptocurrency ecosystem evolves, the exploration of use cases and adoption potential remains an integral component of the journey toward informed and strategic investments.

CHAPTER IV

Technical Analysis for Crypto Investments

Introduction to Technical Analysis

In the dynamic realm of cryptocurrency investments, making informed decisions is a paramount skill. Amidst the inherent volatility and complexity of the cryptocurrency market, technical analysis emerges as a powerful tool for navigating uncertainties and making well-grounded investment choices. This concept is based on forecasting future price changes by analyzing historical price and volume data. Its foundational principle assumes that market prices encapsulate all pertinent information, and patterns and trends that have manifested in the past might replicate in the future. Technical analysts strive to predict price movements and identify potential entry and exit opportunities for their investments by closely examining these patterns and trends.

At its essence, technical analysis rests on the foundation that historical price and trading volume data hold valuable insights into a cryptocurrency's future price direction. This approach operates under the premise that market prices reflect all pertinent information, and patterns and trends observed in the past could recur in the future. By interpreting these patterns and trends, technical analysts seek to predict price movements and identify opportune moments for investment.

The core components of technical analysis encompass trends, support, and resistance levels. Trends denote the general direction in which a cryptocurrency's price is headed, be it upward (bullish), downward (bearish), or sideways (neutral). Identifying trends is a cornerstone of technical analysis, as they offer insights into the prevailing market sentiment. Support and resistance levels represent critical price points that can influence a cryptocurrency's price movements. Support is where the price tends to halt its decline and potentially reverse, while resistance is where it tends to halt its ascent. Recognizing these levels aids in making judicious decisions regarding buying (at support) or selling (at resistance).

Technical analysts rely on a toolkit of indicators and oscillators to complement their analysis. These tools quantify various aspects of price and volume movements, offering supplementary insights. Moving averages, for instance, smooth out price data to expose underlying trends. Relative Strength Index and also Moving Average Convergence Divergence are oscillators that help identify overbought and oversold conditions and potential trend reversals.

Chart patterns further enrich the insights provided by technical analysis. Formations such as triangles, head and shoulders, and double tops/bottoms are patterns derived from historical price movements. These patterns offer indications of potential trend continuations or reversals, assisting investors in anticipating future scenarios.

Applying technical analysis to cryptocurrency investments entails a multifaceted approach encompassing chart patterns, utilizing indicators and oscillators, and discerning confirmation signals. Investors and traders deploy these tools to identify entry and exit points, manage risks, and make informed decisions. However, it's crucial to recognize that technical analysis has limitations. The market is influenced by a plethora of factors, including external news, regulatory changes, and macroeconomic trends. Thus, technical analysis proves most effective when used in conjunction with fundamental analysis and a comprehensive grasp of broader market dynamics.

In cryptocurrency investments, technical analysis intertwines art and science, offering a systematic approach to navigating the market's intricacies. Through the examination of historical price and volume data, technical analysts endeavor to unravel patterns, trends, and pivotal levels that offer insights into future price movements. Investors can enhance their decision-making prowess by grasping trends, identifying support and resistance levels, and leveraging indicators and oscillators. However, it's essential to acknowledge that technical analysis does not encompass unforeseen events or fundamental shifts. Pairing technical analysis with fundamental analysis and a holistic awareness of market dynamics empowers investors to cultivate a comprehensive perspective.

In essence, technical analysis emerges as an invaluable tool within the arsenal of a cryptocurrency investor. It presents a structured approach to interpreting price movements and envisaging market trends. By mastering the tenets of technical analysis, investors can augment their capacity to navigate the volatile cryptocurrency landscape and make choices aligned with their financial aspirations. As the crypto market evolves, the role of technical analysis endures as a source of insight amid the ever-changing currents of digital assets.

Reading Crypto Charts: Common Patterns and Indicators

In the intricate world of cryptocurrency trading, the ability to decipher crypto charts emerges as an essential skill for investors seeking to make well-informed decisions. These charts, which visually represent the historical price movements of digital assets over time, hold a wealth of insights into market trends, patterns, and potential price directions. As the cryptocurrency market is characterized by its inherent volatility, understanding the language of charts becomes an indispensable tool that empowers traders to navigate its unpredictable waters. In this section, we delve into the art of reading crypto charts, unraveling the significance of common patterns and indicators that serve as guiding lights through the complex and ever-changing landscape of cryptocurrency trading.

The visual representation of crypto charts extends beyond mere price fluctuations. These charts reflect the collective psychology of market participants, encapsulating emotions ranging from fear to greed and from euphoria to panic. Within these visual narratives lie encoded patterns and trends that hold the key to anticipating potential future price movements.

Candlestick charts, a popular choice among traders, vividly illustrate price dynamics. Each candlestick encapsulates the price movement during a specific time interval, revealing the opening, closing, highest, and lowest prices. The body of the candlestick, colored differently based on whether the price increased or decreased during that interval, symbolizes the price range between the opening and closing prices. The wicks, also known as shadows, extending from the top and bottom of the body, represent the range between the highest and lowest prices.

The "Head and Shoulders" pattern is a prominent signal of a potential trend reversal among the array of chart patterns. It presents a peak (the head) flanked by two lower peaks (the shoulders), indicating a shift from bullish sentiment to a bearish outlook. "Double Top" and "Double Bottom" patterns are equally noteworthy. The former typically emerges after a substantial price uptrend, implying a potential reversal to a downtrend. Conversely, the latter appears after a prolonged downtrend and signifies the possibility of a reversal to an uptrend. Recognizing and interpreting these patterns equips traders with insights into potential trend changes, allowing them to make strategic decisions.

Indicators serve as essential tools for dissecting price data and extracting hidden insights. Moving Averages, for instance, offer a smoothed representation of price fluctuations, revealing underlying trends. The Relative Strength Index (RSI) functions as an oscillator that indicates whether a cryptocurrency is overbought or oversold. RSI values above 70 indicate overbought conditions, while values below 30 suggest oversold conditions, potentially indicating imminent trend reversals. Another critical indicator, the Moving Average Convergence Divergence (MACD), combines moving averages to spotlight potential shifts in momentum. Divergence between the MACD line and the price trend often serves as a harbinger of potential trend changes.

Fibonacci retracement levels, derived from the Fibonacci sequence, provide a framework for identifying potential support and resistance levels. By illustrating these levels on a chart, traders can anticipate potential price reversals or continuations based on historical price movements.

These retracement levels, including 38.2%, 50%, and 61.8%, serve as significant markers for analyzing price trends and identifying potential reversal points.

Comprehensive chart analysis involves the amalgamation of various elements for a holistic understanding. Traders frequently integrate candlestick patterns, chart patterns, and indicators to validate their hypotheses and make well-considered decisions. For instance, if a cryptocurrency's price approaches a historical resistance level while simultaneously displaying overbought conditions on the RSI, it could indicate an impending price reversal.

However, it's paramount to acknowledge that while chart analysis provides valuable insights, it isn't immune to unexpected market events, sudden news releases, or abrupt shifts in investor sentiment. Therefore, combining chart analysis with fundamental insights and a grasp of broader market dynamics offers a more resilient approach to trading.

In conclusion, reading crypto charts is an art that transcends mere numbers and price movements. It's an expedition into the collective psyche of market participants, a journey to decode trends, patterns, and potential price directions. As cryptocurrencies continue to captivate global attention, the ability to analyze charts remains a potent tool for traders navigating this dynamic landscape. By mastering the language of charts, traders equip themselves with a lens that unveils the intricacies of market sentiment and guides their investment choices. Nevertheless, chart analysis is a skill that demands practice, persistence, and adaptability. It marries technical insights with a nuanced understanding of the broader market ecosystem. As the crypto market evolves, the ability to read and interpret charts becomes an invaluable asset for traders striving to navigate the ebbs and flows of volatility. While charts may not provide all the answers, they offer a profound glimpse into the multifaceted world of crypto trading—a realm where patterns materialize, trends unfold, and opportunities await those with the ability to truly decipher the cryptic language of the market canvas.

Identifying Entry and Exit Points

In the dynamic landscape of cryptocurrency investments, the ability to pinpoint optimal entry and exit points is a defining skill that distinguishes successful investors. The volatility inherent in the crypto market accentuates the significance of timing, where making the right moves at the right times can spell the difference between substantial gains and significant losses. Amid this fluid environment, the art of identifying precise entry and exit points requires a synthesis of analysis, intuition, and a profound understanding of market intricacies. In this section, we delve into the pivotal realm of recognizing entry and exit points in crypto investments, shedding light on the methodologies, considerations, and strategies that guide investors toward sound decisions.

The essence of timing within cryptocurrency trading cannot be overstated. The juncture at which one enters or exits a trade holds immense weight, capable of altering the trajectory of an investment. The inherent volatility of the crypto market amplifies the significance of this timing, as prices can experience remarkable fluctuations within short spans. The art of identifying optimal entry and exit points is forged at the intersection of technical analysis, fundamental insights, and an intuitive grasp of market psychology.

The quest for an optimal entry point commences with a meticulous evaluation of potential investment opportunities. In this pursuit, technical analysis serves as an indispensable tool, enabling investors to dissect historical price movements, chart patterns, and indicators. Identifying trends, recognizing patterns, and discerning support levels are foundational in locating promising entry positions. For instance, opting to buy during a retracement within an overarching uptrend or near a historically significant support level can yield a favorable risk-reward ratio.

Fundamental analysis is equally instrumental in shaping entry decisions. Gaining insight into a cryptocurrency's underlying technology, practical applications, partnerships, and market demand contributes to gauging its long-term viability. The amalgamation of technical and fundamental insights equips investors with a comprehensive foundation upon which to base their entry choices.

Investor sentiment, often swayed by market news, wields a potent influence. Positive developments, such as project development advancements or strategic partnerships, can catalyze price surges, impacting the optimal entry window. Vigilance in monitoring social media platforms, crypto news outlets, and the prevailing community sentiment provides a valuable gauge of market sentiment.

The art of determining exit points is just as crucial as entering a trade at the right moment. Successful exit strategies hinge on comprehending potential price movements, setting predefined profit targets, and skillfully managing risks. Here again, technical analysis occupies a pivotal role as traders assess trends, resistance levels, and plausible price ceilings. Opting to sell near resistance levels or during overbought conditions signaled by indicators like the Relative Strength Index (RSI) can shield accumulated gains.

Established based on individual investment goals, profit targets are integral to effective exit strategies. Gradually taking profits off the table as the price attains specific milestones strikes a balance between securing gains and leaving room for further upward movement.

A prudent exit strategy inherently involves risk management. The placement of stop-loss orders, which trigger sales once the price reaches a designated threshold, acts as a safeguard against substantial losses. This pragmatic approach prevents emotions from driving decisions during periods of heightened market turbulence.

Investors employ diverse strategies in the pursuit of entry and exit points. Scalping involves swift trading to capitalize on minor price fluctuations, typically executed within short timeframes. Day trading entails concluding trades within a single day, seeking to exploit intraday price volatility. Swing trading aims to capture price movements spanning several days or weeks. In contrast, long-term investors adopt a patient stance, holding assets for extended durations with an eye on capitalizing on substantial gains over time.

The prevailing market conditions play a pivotal role in shaping traders' strategies. Bull markets, characterized by sustained upward price trends, provide ample opportunities for purchasing during price corrections and capitalizing on the upward momentum. Conversely, bear markets warrant a cautious approach, with strategies that prioritize loss mitigation over profit maximization.

The psychology of investors interweaves with the process of identifying entry and exit points. Emotions, ranging from fear to greed, can influence decision-making and prompt impulsive actions. Developing a disciplined approach that adheres to predetermined criteria mitigates the sway of emotional turbulence.

Inherent in the realm of identifying entry and exit points is an essential virtue—patience. Waiting for conditions that align with one's strategy often proves more rewarding than hastily executing trades driven by the FOMO (fear of missing out). Similarly, adhering to profit targets guards against the inclination to retain assets for too long, thereby risking the forfeiture of accrued gains.

In conclusion, the ability to identify optimal entry and exit points in crypto investments encompasses an intricate interplay of analysis, strategy, and self-discipline. The aptness of timing—often the fulcrum on which success pivots—demands a holistic approach that integrates technical analysis, fundamental insights, market sentiment, and the judicious management of risk. Astute investors acknowledge that while timing is pivotal, it is also riddled with challenges. The dynamic nature and unpredictability of the crypto market elevate each decision to the status of a calculated risk.

As the landscape of cryptocurrencies evolves, the capacity to discern entry and exit points remains a linchpin skill. A judicious investor harnesses this skill to navigate the undulating waves of the market with poise, capitalizing on opportunities, preserving gains, and effectively mitigating risks. The precision of timing stands as a testament to the intricate world of crypto investments—a world in which analysis harmonizes with intuition, strategy intertwines with self-control, and the prospect of rewards aligns harmoniously with the discernment of the right moments to enter and exit the market.

Managing Risk with Stop-Loss and Take-Profit Orders

Prudent risk management takes center stage in the electrifying domain of cryptocurrency investments, where the allure of rapid gains coexists with the volatility that underpins the market. Within this context, the deployment of stop-loss and take-profit orders emerges as a linchpin strategy for astute investors. These orders wield the power to guide and safeguard investments, offering a structured approach to minimize potential losses and lock in profits. In this section, we delve into the artistry of managing risk with stop-loss and take- profit orders in the world of crypto investments, unveiling their mechanisms, the advantages they confer, and the strategic considerations that inform sagacious decision-making.

At the heart of this risk management approach lies the comprehension of stop-loss orders, a tool tailored to navigate the tumultuous terrain of market volatility. Acting as a preemptive measure, these orders stipulate a predefined price level below the prevailing market rate. When the cryptocurrency's price intersects or plunges beneath this marked threshold, the stop-loss order springs into action, executing a sell order that curbs the losses by avoiding further depreciation beyond the pre-established limit. This mechanism acknowledges the swift and unpredictable fluctuations inherent in the crypto domain, proffering a shield against minor setbacks snowballing into monumental losses. By setting a predetermined cap on the acceptable loss, investors relinquish the emotional toll of making rash decisions during phases of market turbulence.

In parallel to this, the implementation of take-profit orders assumes the role of a calculated protector of gains. Guided by a similar principle of advance planning, take- profit orders trigger once the price attains or surpasses a predetermined level above the present market value. An automatic sell order is executed upon activation, affording investors the luxury of locking in gains before the price potentially retraces. This approach is a counterbalance to the natural inclination to clutch assets for extended durations, driven by the hopeful anticipation of further appreciation. By establishing predefined exit points for profit realization, investors traverse the market with a heightened degree of objectivity, reaping rewards while sheltering themselves from the capriciousness of price fluctuations.

The interplay of these risk management strategies, namely stop-loss and take-profit orders, furnishes investors with a versatile toolkit for shaping their investment narrative. This duality finds its greatest advantage for traders who may not possess the luxury of real-time market monitoring. Investors construct a dynamic scaffold that guides their investment trajectory even in their absence by weaving a cohesive fabric of these two orders.

The linchpin of this synergistic approach is the establishment of an equilibrium between the degree of risk and the prospects of reward. The positioning of stop-loss orders necessitates meticulous calibration; setting them too proximate to the entry price risks premature selling due to the volatility-induced market noise, while placing them too far distanced exposes investments to greater peril. A similar philosophy dictates the setting of take-profit levels. Striking a harmonious balance between conservatism and ambition prevents the imposition of unwarranted limitations on gains or the premature offloading of assets.

The strategic tailoring of these orders pivots on individual investment goals and risk thresholds. Long-term investors, intent on weathering the ebbs and flows of market undulations, might opt for wider stop-loss margins to avoid being prematurely ejected from positions. Conversely, short-term traders, with a heightened sensitivity to fleeting market shifts, might embrace tighter stop-loss thresholds to curtail potential losses promptly.

Akin to the tailored nature of these strategies, take-profit levels also reflect individualized considerations. The long-term investor's purview could encompass a graduated series of take-profit levels, each tethered to a distinct milestone. This approach effectively enables the investor to savor gains progressively without prematurely relinquishing their assets. Conversely, short-term traders might adopt more immediate take-profit targets, capitalizing on the rapid fluctuations that typify intraday price movements.

In this risk management saga, the role of investor mindfulness and flexibility must be considered. While the implementation of stop-loss and take-profit orders is indispensable, the fluidity of market dynamics remains omnipresent. Unexpected news releases, shifts in investor sentiment, or regulatory modifications can precipitate swift price oscillations, potentially rendering these orders subject to deviations. Thus, investors are well-advised to maintain a vigilant watchfulness and a readiness to recalibrate their strategies in response to the unfolding landscape.

The significance of stop-loss and take-profit orders extends beyond their mechanical execution. These tools resonate profoundly with the psychological underpinnings of trading. The omnipresent emotions of fear and greed, known to impede rational judgment, find their equilibrium in these orders. Through the preconceived structuring of these orders, investors mitigate the sway of emotional tumult, rendering their decision-making more lucid and calculated even in the throes of market upheaval.

The establishment of these orders assumes the role of discipline, curbing the impulse to succumb to emotional whims during phases of market turbulence. This disciplined framework aligns with the overarching aspiration of engendering rational decisions that are consonant with the predetermined strategies.

In conclusion, the management of risk through the art of stop-loss and take-profit orders constitutes an intricate choreography within the realm of cryptocurrency investments. These tools stand as sentinels, wielding the power to shield against losses and amplify gains. Through the strategic deployment of these mechanisms, investors retain a modicum of control within a landscape renowned for its capriciousness.

Nevertheless, the orchestration of these orders is not devoid of challenges. The crypto market remains a stage where the unforeseen remains an ever-present player, capable of subverting even the most well-conceived plans. Thus, the harmonization of these tools with an encompassing comprehension of market trends, fundamental insights, and unwavering vigilance persists as the compass guiding investors toward optimal outcomes.

As the trajectory of the cryptocurrency landscape continues its dynamic evolution, the prudence of risk management, encapsulated in the sagacity of stop-loss and take-profit orders, retains its prominence. Investors who tread this intricate terrain with judiciousness, who grasp both the potential rewards and lurking risks, are poised to navigate the terrain adeptly. Such investors adeptly seize opportunities, shield their investments, and adroitly balance the dichotomy of ambition and circumspection as they journey through the captivating realm of crypto investments.

CHAPTER V

Diversification and Portfolio Management

The Importance of Diversification in Crypto Investments

In the ever-evolving landscape of cryptocurrency investments, diversification emerges as a beacon of wisdom, offering a strategic approach that has proven its worth across various investment domains. Diversification is a safeguard against the unpredictable nature of the crypto market, characterized by its rapid price fluctuations and dynamic trends. Instead of concentrating investments in one business, diversification spreads them over a variety of assets. This practice is rooted in the fundamental principle of risk mitigation—the idea that by allocating resources among multiple assets, the impact of poor performance from any individual asset is lessened on the overall portfolio.

Within cryptocurrencies, where volatility is a defining characteristic, diversification takes on added significance. The potential for substantial gains is balanced by the equally potent potential for significant losses. In this context, relying solely on one cryptocurrency is akin to placing all eggs in a single basket—a strategy fraught with risk. Diversification becomes an antidote to this vulnerability. By distributing investments across multiple cryptocurrencies, investors shield themselves from the disproportionate impact of a single asset's downturn. While the gains from certain assets might offset the losses incurred by others, the overarching result is a more balanced and resilient portfolio.

Diversification strategies within the crypto landscape encompass a range of approaches. One avenue involves diversifying across different types of cryptocurrencies, capitalizing on the varied characteristics and market behaviors of each. Bitcoin, Ethereum, and alternative coins (altcoins) each offer distinct use cases and price trajectories, allowing for exposure to multiple facets of the crypto market. Beyond cryptocurrencies, diversification can extend to traditional assets like stocks and bonds, adding an element of stability to a portfolio otherwise subject to the pronounced volatility of cryptocurrencies.

The benefits of diversification extend beyond risk mitigation. This practice could enhance portfolio performance by capturing the growth opportunities presented by various market segments. If one cryptocurrency experiences a surge, its gains can contribute positively to the overall portfolio, mitigating the impact of stagnant or slightly fluctuating assets.

However, diversification has challenges. Over-diversification, the act of spreading investments too thinly across numerous assets, can dilute potential gains and complicate portfolio management. Individual risk tolerance and investing objectives must be carefully taken into account in order to strike the correct balance between risk reduction and the potential for profits. Additionally, the fluid nature of the crypto market demands continuous vigilance and adjustment to ensure that the portfolio remains aligned with prevailing market trends and developments.

In conclusion, the importance of diversification in crypto investments is a cardinal principle that underscores the pragmatic approach to navigating the uncertainties of the cryptocurrency market. Beyond being a risk management strategy, diversification encapsulates a forward-looking perspective that acknowledges the crypto market's allure, its inherent risks, and the potential for growth. As this domain continues to evolve, diversification remains a steadfast companion, guiding investors through the dynamic currents of the crypto landscape with the wisdom of balance, prudence, and a strategic focus on building resilient and rewarding portfolios.

Building a Balanced Crypto Portfolio

In the intricate world of cryptocurrency investments, crafting a balanced portfolio emerges as a pivotal strategy that harmonizes this dynamic market's inherent risks and rewards. This process transcends mere asset accumulation; it's a deliberate orchestration of diversification, thoughtful allocation, and risk management that mirrors the principles of traditional finance. At its core, building a balanced crypto portfolio revolves around the recognition that the crypto realm is a realm of volatility and unpredictability, necessitating a calculated approach that aligns with individual goals and risk tolerance.

Central to this endeavor is the principle of diversification, which serves as the cornerstone of risk mitigation. The volatile nature of cryptocurrencies makes them susceptible to rapid price swings and unforeseen market developments. Diversification involves distributing investments across different types of cryptocurrencies, reducing the impact of a poor-performing asset on the overall portfolio. This practice shields investors from overexposure to the fortunes of a single asset and enhances the portfolio's resilience.

Strategic asset allocation and weighting are the pillars of a balanced crypto portfolio. The allocation process involves determining how much of the portfolio is allocated to various cryptocurrencies and potentially other asset classes. This decision hinges on individual risk appetite, investment goals, and market outlook. Portfolios often diversify among established core cryptocurrencies like Bitcoin and Ethereum, established altcoins, and possibly more speculative emerging projects. Weighting, the proportion of the portfolio allocated to each cryptocurrency, is a delicate equilibrium. Factors like market capitalization, growth potential, and risk influence this decision. The objective is to avoid overemphasizing any one asset while optimizing returns and managing risks.

The interplay of correlation, the measure of price movement alignment between assets, adds another layer of sophistication to portfolio construction. Including assets with low correlation can insulate the portfolio against simultaneous price swings, enhancing stability. Understanding correlation and incorporating assets with varying profiles becomes a prudent risk management strategy as the crypto market operates with its unique dynamics.

Balancing risk and reward is a tightrope act influenced by investment horizons. Long-term investors might lean towards a more conservative allocation, focusing on established cryptocurrencies with proven track records. In contrast, short-term approaches might encompass a calculated mix of established and emerging projects, where the pursuit of higher returns is coupled with heightened risks.

Maintaining a balanced crypto portfolio is not a one-time endeavor; it's an ongoing process of adaptation. The cryptocurrency landscape is perpetually evolving, with new projects entering the scene and market trends shifting. Regular portfolio rebalancing ensures alignment with current market conditions and the investor's goals. This could entail adjusting asset weights or even integrating new cryptocurrencies that resonate with the evolving market.

Building a balanced crypto portfolio is an art that harmonizes strategy, analysis, and ongoing vigilance in the grand symphony of investment. It's a testament to an investor's ability to navigate the nuances of the crypto market with sagacity, embracing opportunities while tempering risks. The importance of a balanced portfolio amplifies as the cryptocurrency ecosystem continues its rapid expansion. This project is ultimately a synthesis of innovation and caution, connecting with growth aspirations and strengthened resilience in the face of a constantly shifting crypto ecosystem.

Rebalancing Strategies and Frequency

In cryptocurrency investments, where volatility is the norm and market dynamics can swiftly shift, the practice of portfolio rebalancing emerges as a strategic compass that guides investors toward maintaining alignment with their desired risk and return profiles. Rebalancing is a methodical process that involves readjusting the allocation of assets within a portfolio to bring it back to its intended target. As cryptocurrencies surge and retreat with notable frequency, the art of rebalancing has gained prominence as a mechanism to manage risk, capture gains, and preserve the portfolio's desired composition.

The purpose of rebalancing is to restore a portfolio's original risk and return characteristics. Over time, as asset prices fluctuate, the proportion of assets within a portfolio can deviate from the intended allocation. This deviation could expose the portfolio to higher or lower risk levels than initially intended. Rebalancing aims to mitigate this risk by selling assets that have appreciated significantly and reinvesting the proceeds into underperforming assets, ensuring that the portfolio remains consistent with the investor's risk appetite and objectives.

Two primary strategies govern the process of rebalancing: time-based and threshold-based. The time-based strategy involves rebalancing at regular intervals, such as quarterly or annually, regardless of how much the portfolio's asset allocation has shifted. This approach offers simplicity and automation, helping investors stick to a disciplined rebalancing schedule. On the other hand, the threshold-based strategy focuses on specific target thresholds for each asset class. Rebalancing is triggered when an asset's allocation deviates from its target threshold by a predefined percentage. This strategy is more responsive to market movements and can prevent the portfolio from drifting significantly from its intended allocation.

Determining how often to rebalance a crypto portfolio hinges on several factors. A critical consideration is the level of market volatility. In the crypto space, where asset prices can experience wild swings within short periods, more frequent rebalancing might be prudent to prevent substantial deviations from the intended allocation. However, frequent rebalancing can also result in increased transaction costs and administrative overhead.

Investors should also evaluate their tolerance for risk and their investment horizon. Short-term investors seeking quick gains might opt for more frequent rebalancing to seize opportunities and minimize risk exposure. Long-term investors aiming for steady growth and stability may opt for less frequent rebalancing to avoid unnecessary trading fees and taxes associated with frequent portfolio adjustments.

The advent of technology has empowered investors with tools for automating the rebalancing process. Automated platforms can track asset performance and trigger rebalancing when predefined thresholds are breached. This reduces the burden of constant monitoring and ensures that the portfolio stays in line with the intended allocation even in the face of rapid market changes.

Nonetheless, automation doesn't negate the importance of vigilance. While automated systems streamline the process, investors should regularly review and adjust the rebalancing parameters to account for changing market conditions and individual goals.

Rebalancing in the context of crypto investments is an art that marries strategy with adaptability. It requires a delicate balance between maintaining portfolio alignment and minimizing transaction costs. The right strategy and frequency depend on the investor's risk tolerance, investment horizon, and market outlook.

Ultimately, the rebalancing practice underscores the cryptocurrency landscape's dynamic nature. It empowers investors to navigate the inherent volatility while adhering to their desired investment trajectories. As the crypto market evolves and new projects emerge, the judicious application of rebalancing strategies and frequency is a key tool in achieving a portfolio that resonates with growth aspirations, risk management, and resilience in the face of ever-changing market tides.

Tracking and Measuring Portfolio Performance

In cryptocurrency investments, where market dynamics can shift dramatically within minutes, the ability to track and measure portfolio performance takes on heightened importance. The crypto landscape is characterized by volatility, innovation, and rapid change, making diligent monitoring a crucial practice for investors seeking to navigate this dynamic space successfully.

At its essence, performance tracking is about gaining insights that transcend mere numbers. While the primary goal is to gauge the financial progress of an investment portfolio, effective tracking goes beyond raw returns. It involves understanding the factors that drive those returns, evaluating the effectiveness of investment decisions, and refining strategies based on empirical evidence. Performance tracking serves as a compass that directs investors through the complexities of the unpredictable crypto market, where values can vary rapidly, and helps them stay on course even in challenging times.

Performance metrics in crypto investments encompass a spectrum of measures that provide a comprehensive view of portfolio health. While gains and losses are fundamental metrics, risk-adjusted returns offer a more nuanced perspective. Metrics like the Sharpe ratio assess how well the portfolio's returns compensate for the risks taken. A higher Sharpe ratio indicates better risk-adjusted returns. The Sortino ratio focuses on downside risk, which is particularly relevant in the crypto market, where sudden downturns can be pronounced. These metrics aid in evaluating whether the returns achieved are commensurate with the level of risk undertaken.

Benchmarking against market indices provides a broader context for evaluating portfolio performance. Crypto-specific indices, such as the Crypto Fear & Greed Index and the Bloomberg Galaxy Crypto Index, offer insights into market sentiment and sector-wide trends. Comparing portfolio performance to these benchmarks can reveal whether gains and losses are due to individual decisions or are reflective of broader market trends. This contextualization is crucial for distinguishing between alpha—the excess return earned compared to the market—and beta—the sensitivity of the portfolio's returns to market movements.

Measuring and tracking portfolio performance in the crypto market comes with its own set of challenges. The decentralized nature of cryptocurrencies and the absence of a standardized reporting framework can lead to inconsistencies in data collection and reporting. Moreover, the 24/7 trading nature of the crypto market requires constant vigilance, as portfolio values can change even when traditional financial markets are closed.

Technology has emerged as a valuable ally in pursuing accurate portfolio performance tracking. Cryptocurrency portfolio tracking platforms offer real-time updates, historical data, and graphical representations of performance trends. These platforms consolidate data from various exchanges and wallets, providing a comprehensive overview of an investor's holdings. Moreover, automation tools can assist in aggregating data, calculating performance metrics, and generating performance reports. Such precision is essential in a market where timing and accuracy can significantly impact investment outcomes.

In conclusion, tracking and measuring portfolio performance in crypto investments is a multi-faceted endeavor that goes beyond surface-level gains and losses. It's about gaining insights, refining strategies, and making informed decisions in the face of a volatile and rapidly evolving market. Performance metrics offer a lens through which investors can assess risk-adjusted returns, while benchmarking provides context within the broader crypto landscape. Challenges and technological solutions highlight the unique nature of the crypto market's data landscape. By embracing these practices, investors can navigate the dynamic currents of the crypto realm with clarity and confidence, leveraging the power of data to steer their investments toward success.

CHAPTER VI

Navigating Regulatory and Security Challenges

Regulatory Landscape for Cryptocurrencies

The rapid rise of cryptocurrencies has ushered in a new era of finance, offering innovative opportunities and challenges. As these digital assets gained prominence, governments and regulatory bodies around the world grappled with the complexities of overseeing an industry that transcends traditional financial boundaries. The regulatory landscape for cryptocurrencies is a dynamic tapestry woven with a patchwork of approaches, reflecting diverse attitudes toward innovation, risk, and the need for consumer protection. In this section, we delve into the intricate web of cryptocurrency regulations, examining the motivations behind regulatory efforts, the challenges they entail, and the evolving global perspective on this decentralized revolution.

Governments' motivations for regulating cryptocurrencies are multifaceted. While some nations approach this realm with caution due to concerns about money laundering, tax evasion, and fraud, others recognize the potential for economic growth, technological advancement, and financial inclusion that cryptocurrencies can bring. Regulatory efforts often strive to balance fostering innovation and safeguarding financial systems.

A defining challenge in the regulatory landscape is the classification of cryptocurrencies. Are they securities subject to securities regulations, or are they digital currencies falling under the purview of monetary authorities? This classification determines the regulatory framework these assets are subject to, impacting taxation, trading, and reporting requirements. The absence of a universally agreed-upon classification has led to varying interpretations and regulations worldwide.

The regulatory landscape for cryptocurrencies varies significantly from one country to another. Some nations have embraced these digital assets, creating friendly environments for innovation through clear regulations. Others have taken a more cautious approach, implementing strict measures to curb potential risks. While countries like Japan have enacted comprehensive legal frameworks to license and regulate cryptocurrency exchanges, others like China have banned initial coin offerings (ICOs) and restricted crypto trading. This divergence highlights the complexities of finding common ground in a decentralized landscape.

A common regulatory focus across jurisdictions revolves around combating money laundering and ensuring Know Your Customer (KYC) compliance. Cryptocurrency exchanges and businesses are often required to implement rigorous customer identification procedures, mirroring those of traditional financial institutions. These measures seek to prevent illicit activities while providing a level of consumer protection.

The United States has been a focal point for cryptocurrency regulation. Regulatory bodies such as Commodity Futures Trading Commission (CFTC) and Securities and Exchange Commission (SEC) grapple with defining cryptocurrencies and determining their regulatory status. The lack of uniformity in approach across federal agencies has led to ambiguity, which the industry seeks to address through lobbying efforts and engagement with policymakers.

The borderless nature of cryptocurrencies poses challenges for regulators. A regulation implemented in one country can impact the global crypto ecosystem, as transactions and investments transcend geographical boundaries. This has led to discussions about international cooperation to harmonize regulations and prevent regulatory arbitrage.

The regulatory landscape for cryptocurrencies is still in its early stages and is expected to evolve. Striking the right balance between fostering innovation, consumer protection, and risk mitigation remains an ongoing challenge. Industry participants, policymakers, and regulatory bodies continue to engage in dialogues, seeking to establish coherent frameworks that promote responsible growth while mitigating potential threats.

In conclusion, the regulatory landscape for cryptocurrencies is a multifaceted mosaic, reflective of the diverse global perspectives on innovation and risk. While some nations embrace these digital assets with open arms, others exercise caution, leading to a patchwork of approaches. The classification dilemma, security concerns, and the need for international cooperation underscore the complexities of overseeing a decentralized and borderless industry. As cryptocurrencies continue to reshape finance, the quest for balanced and effective regulation continues—an ongoing journey that navigates the uncharted waters of technological disruption and financial transformation.

Compliance and Tax Considerations

As cryptocurrencies gain traction and become a fixture in financial landscapes worldwide, compliance and taxation have taken center stage. The unique nature of these digital assets has spurred a complex web of regulations, guidelines, and taxation frameworks that seek to govern their use, trade, and reporting. The evolving nature of the crypto ecosystem presents challenges for individuals, businesses, and regulatory bodies alike, as they grapple with the intricacies of compliance and the determination of tax liabilities. This section delves into the multifaceted world of compliance and tax considerations for cryptocurrencies, shedding light on the regulatory landscape, challenges, and emerging trends.

The decentralized nature of cryptocurrencies has posed significant challenges for regulatory bodies seeking to establish comprehensive compliance frameworks. The lack of a centralized authority and the borderless nature of crypto transactions create hurdles in enforcing regulatory standards uniformly. As a result, countries have adopted diverse approaches—some have embraced cryptocurrencies, while others have been more cautious, imposing stringent regulations to mitigate risks such as money laundering, fraud, and consumer protection.

Compliance in the crypto space often centers around Know Your Customer (KYC) as well as Anti-Money Laundering (AML) regulations. Cryptocurrency exchanges and businesses are increasingly required to implement KYC procedures, ensuring users' identities are verified to prevent illicit activities. AML regulations are particularly critical, given the perceived potential for cryptocurrencies to assist money laundering and other financial crimes. Implementing effective KYC and AML measures aims to create a safer ecosystem while instilling accountability within the crypto industry.

Determining the tax treatment of cryptocurrencies has been a perplexing challenge. The question of whether cryptocurrencies should be treated as currency or property has far-reaching implications for tax obligations. When sold or exchanged, cryptocurrencies may be subject to capital gains tax in some jurisdictions since they are regarded as property. In others, they are treated as currency, potentially leading to more complex tax implications for day-to-day transactions. The lack of standardized global guidelines has resulted in varying interpretations and tax treatments.

The decentralized nature of cryptocurrencies can create challenges in tracking and reporting transactions for tax purposes. Unlike traditional financial systems, where intermediaries facilitate reporting, cryptocurrencies often involve peer-to-peer transactions that may not be immediately traceable. This poses challenges for tax authorities seeking to ensure accurate reporting and collection of taxes owed.

The cryptocurrency ecosystem's meteoric expansion has prompted an evolution in taxation systems. Some countries have opted for lenient taxation policies to encourage innovation, while others have chosen to impose more stringent regulations to safeguard financial stability. The lack of global consistency has prompted discussions about the need for international cooperation to harmonize taxation approaches, thereby minimizing regulatory arbitrage.

As the cryptocurrency industry matures, regulatory bodies are striving for greater clarity in compliance and taxation frameworks. The rise of decentralized finance

(DeFi) and non-fungible tokens (NFTs) has further complicated the regulatory landscape. Governments are now working to develop regulatory frameworks that encompass these new digital asset classes, addressing their unique characteristics and potential risks.

In conclusion, compliance and taxation considerations for cryptocurrencies represent an intricate interplay between technology, finance, and regulation. The global regulatory landscape is evolving rapidly, responding to the growing influence of cryptocurrencies in the mainstream economy. The challenges of ensuring KYC/AML compliance, determining tax treatment, and tracking transactions underscore the complexities individuals, businesses, and regulatory bodies face. As the crypto industry continues redefining finance, pursuing balanced and effective compliance and taxation frameworks remains an ongoing journey—one that navigates the dynamic currents of innovation, accountability, and regulatory adaptation.

Security Best Practices: Protecting Your Investments

In cryptocurrencies, where decentralized finance converges with cutting-edge technology, security emerges as a paramount concern. The digital nature of these assets and the absence of traditional intermediaries make them susceptible to unique security risks. Strong security measures are essential as a result of the rise in cyberattacks, scams, and fraud attempts brought on by cryptocurrency. Protecting your investments in cryptocurrencies requires a comprehensive understanding of security best practices encompassing wallet management, online behavior, and safeguarding personal information. This section delves into the critical landscape of security practices that empower investors to navigate the crypto realm safely.

At the heart of cryptocurrency security lies wallet management. Wallets serve as digital vaults for storing and managing your cryptocurrencies. Understanding the distinction between hot wallets (online) and cold wallets (offline) is crucial. Hot wallets offer convenience for frequent transactions, but they are more susceptible to hacking. On the other hand, cold wallets provide enhanced security by keeping your assets offline. A sort of cold wallet known as a hardware wallet gives you a physical device to keep your private keys, protecting them from online threats. Ensuring strong passwords and two-factor authentication (2FA) adds additional layers of protection to your wallets.

The concept of private keys is central to cryptocurrency security. Your private keys, which provide access to your cryptocurrency, should be securely handled. Never share your private keys with anyone, and avoid storing them on devices connected to the internet. Paper wallets, which involve printing out your private keys, offer a physical form of storage that's less vulnerable to online attacks. Cryptocurrency exchanges often manage private keys on your behalf, but this approach can come with risks, as historical exchange hacks demonstrate.

Phishing attacks and scams are prevalent in the crypto landscape. Cybercriminals use fake websites, emails, and social media accounts to trick users into revealing their private keys or sending funds. Be cautious of unsolicited communications, double-check website URLs, and verify the authenticity of accounts before engaging. Always initiate transactions and interactions from trusted sources.

Ensuring the security of your devices is equally important. Keep your operating systems, software, and antivirus programs updated to protect against vulnerabilities that hackers could exploit. Avoid using public Wi-Fi networks for sensitive activities related to cryptocurrencies, as they can expose your data to potential interception.

Diversification is a fundamental investment strategy, and it also applies to security. Avoid relying on a single access point or a single wallet to store all your cryptocurrencies. To lessen the effects of a potential hack, diversify your assets across several wallets and platforms.

Backing up your wallets and recovery phrases is crucial in case of device loss, damage, or malfunction. Without proper backups, losing access to your wallets could result in the irretrievable loss of your cryptocurrencies. Store backups securely, preferably offline, and ensure that trusted individuals know the location and access procedures for recovery in case of emergencies.

The crypto world is rapidly changing, therefore it's critical to stay up to date on the most recent security risks, industry advancements, and best practices. Engage with reputable sources, forums, and communities to gain insights and share experiences. By being well-informed, you can make wise judgments and efficiently safeguard your investments.

As the world of cryptocurrencies can be complex, seeking guidance from professionals with expertise in security and cryptography can be invaluable. Consult experts, attend workshops, and engage with security-focused communities to learn from those who specialize in securing digital assets.

In conclusion, security best practices are the bedrock of safeguarding your cryptocurrency investments. The digital nature of these assets demands vigilance, awareness, and a proactive approach to minimize risks.

Every step from secure wallet management to continuous education, contributes to a resilient defense against the evolving landscape of cyber threats. By embracing these practices, investors can confidently navigate the crypto terrain, knowing that their assets are protected against the challenges posed by technological innovation and the digital age.

Dealing with Hacks and Scams

In the world of cryptocurrencies, where innovation converges with decentralization, the potential for hacks and scams has emerged as a stark reality. As the popularity of cryptocurrencies grows, so does the ingenuity of cybercriminals seeking to exploit vulnerabilities and deceive unsuspecting investors. The decentralized and pseudonymous nature of cryptocurrencies presents both opportunities and challenges, making it imperative for investors to be equipped with the knowledge and strategies to deal with hacks and scams effectively. In this section, we delve into the complex landscape of cyber threats, providing insights into prevention, response, and mitigation measures to safeguard your crypto investments.

Hacks and scams in the crypto space come in myriad forms, from sophisticated hacking attempts targeting exchanges and wallets to fraudulent schemes promising outsized returns. Phishing attacks, where malicious actors create fake websites and communications to steal sensitive information, are a common vector for scams. Ponzi schemes and initial coin offering (ICO) scams have also preyed on investors' aspirations for quick profits. Understanding the diversity of threats is the first step in developing a proactive defense strategy.

Education and vigilance are the foundation of protecting your investments from hacks and scams. Educate yourself about common tactics used by cybercriminals, such as unsolicited communications, fake social media accounts, and promises of guaranteed returns. Keep up with the most recent risks and recommended procedures by participating in reliable sites, forums, and communities. By being informed, you can recognize red flags and avoid falling victim to scams.

Implementing robust security measures for your cryptocurrency holdings is essential. Utilize reputable wallets with strong encryption and two-factor authentication (2FA) to mitigate unauthorized access. Cold storage solutions, such as hardware wallets, keep your assets offline, reducing exposure to online threats. Regularly update your software, operating systems, and antivirus programs to prevent exploitation of known vulnerabilities.

Selecting reputable cryptocurrency exchanges and platforms is crucial to mitigating the risk of hacks and scams. Conduct thorough research before using an exchange, considering factors such as security features, regulatory compliance, and user reviews. Look for platforms that offer insurance coverage for potential breaches. Additionally, use exchanges that implement cold storage solutions to reduce the risk of online attacks.

Enable multi-factor verification (2FA) wherever possible to add a futher layer of security to your accounts. This requires an additional verification step beyond the password, making unauthorized access significantly more challenging for attackers. Safeguard your private keys— never share them with anyone and avoid storing them on devices connected to the internet.

Swift action is crucial in the unfortunate event of a hack or scam. If you believe someone may have accessed your accounts or wallets without authorization, change your passwords immediately and secure your accounts by enabling 2FA. Contact the respective platform's customer support to report the incident and seek guidance on recovery steps. If you identify a scam or a fraudulent scheme, report it to relevant authorities and platforms to help prevent others from falling victim.

In severe cases of hacking or fraud, seeking assistance from cybersecurity experts and legal professionals can be beneficial. They can help analyze the situation, determine the extent of the damage, and advise on potential recovery options. Reporting incidents to law enforcement agencies may also contribute to tracking down cybercriminals and preventing further harm.

Dealing with hacks and scams in cryptocurrencies is an ongoing journey that demands constant vigilance and adaptability. By staying informed, implementing robust security practices, and making informed choices about exchanges and platforms, you can fortify your digital investments against the evolving landscape of cyber threats. While no approach can provide absolute immunity, proactive measures significantly reduce the risk and empower you to navigate the crypto realm confidently.

In conclusion, the digital age brings unparalleled opportunities and risks, especially in the realm of cryptocurrencies. Hacks and scams are unwelcome companions in this journey, demanding resilience, education, and proactive engagement. By staying informed, securing your assets, and responding swiftly to potential threats, you can position yourself as a vigilant and empowered participant in the cryptocurrency ecosystem—a participant who embraces the promise of innovation while safeguarding against the perils of the digital frontier.

CHAPTER VII

Identifying Promising Cryptocurrencies

Spotlight on Major Cryptocurrencies: Bitcoin, Ethereum, and More

The explosion of cryptocurrencies has given rise to a diverse landscape of digital assets, each with its unique features, use cases, and potential for disruption. Among the multitude of cryptocurrencies, a few have emerged as titans that not only pioneered the movement but continue to influence the trajectory of the entire industry. In this section, we highlight some of the major cryptocurrencies, including Bitcoin, Ethereum, and others, delving into their origins, technological foundations, and their impact on reshaping the financial landscape.

Bitcoin, introduced by an enigmatic figure known as Satoshi Nakamoto in 2008, marked the birth of cryptocurrencies and blockchain technology. It serves as both a digital currency and a decentralized store of value. Operating on a proof-of-work consensus mechanism, Bitcoin's blockchain enables secure and transparent peer-to-peer transactions without the need for intermediaries. Its 21 million coin supply cap and decentralized structure have made it a digital gold standard, with supporters acknowledging its potential as a hedge against traditional financial volatility.

Ethereum, introduced by Vitalik Buterin in 2015, extended the possibilities of blockchain beyond mere transactions. The capacity to create smart contracts and decentralized apps (DApps) is provided by Ethereum, which operates as a decentralized platform. These smart contracts automate and execute predefined actions based on certain conditions, revolutionizing industries such as finance, supply chain, and gaming. Ethereum introduced the concept of gas fees to incentivize miners and secure the network, although concerns about scalability and energy consumption have prompted discussions about transitioning to a proof-of-stake consensus mechanism.

Ripple, introduced in 2012, takes a different approach, aiming to facilitate cross-border payments and remittances. Unlike most cryptocurrencies, Ripple doesn't rely on mining. Instead, its consensus protocol validates transactions through a network of trusted nodes. As a bridge between conventional banking and the blockchain world, Ripple has been positioned as a result of its emphasis on relationships with financial institutions and its digital payment solutions. However, its centralized nature and regulatory challenges have sparked debates about its alignment with the decentralized ethos of cryptocurrencies.

Cardano, founded by Charles Hoskinson in 2017, emphasizes a scientific approach to blockchain development. Built on peer-reviewed research, Cardano aims to offer scalability, interoperability, and sustainability. Its layered architecture separates the settlement and computation layers, allowing for flexible upgrades and improvements. Cardano's approach has garnered attention for its emphasis on research-backed innovation and its commitment to long-term scalability.

Binance Coin, introduced by Binance Exchange in 2017, initially served as a utility token within the Binance platform, offering reduced trading fees. However, it has evolved to become the native asset of the Binance Smart Chain, a parallel blockchain network supporting decentralized applications. BNB's versatility, adoption, and role in Binance's expanding ecosystem have contributed to its popularity.

Polkadot, founded by Ethereum co-founder Gavin Wood, aims to address one of the key challenges in the blockchain space: interoperability. Introduced in 2020, Polkadot facilitates communication between different blockchains, enabling data and value to be shared seamlessly across various networks. Its design focuses on scalability, security, and the ability to upgrade without requiring hard forks.

While Bitcoin and Ethereum remain the giants of the cryptocurrency realm, the ecosystem has expanded to encompass a multitude of projects with diverse applications and visions. Each cryptocurrency reflects its creators' ideologies, technological innovations, and the unique problems they aim to solve. However, the landscape is also marked by volatility, regulatory challenges, and technological shifts that can impact the fortunes of these digital assets.

In conclusion, major cryptocurrencies like Bitcoin and Ethereum, along with other prominent players like Ripple, Cardano, Binance Coin, and Polkadot, have played pivotal roles in shaping the advancement of the digital economy. From the pioneering concept of digital cash to the creation of programmable blockchains and decentralized applications, these cryptocurrencies have spurred innovations that continue to disrupt traditional industries. As the ecosystem evolves and adapts, it's essential to remain mindful of the diverse trajectories and potential impact each cryptocurrency may have on the global financial landscape.

Emerging Altcoins with Potential

The cryptocurrency landscape, once dominated solely by Bitcoin, has evolved into a vibrant ecosystem of diverse digital assets, often referred to as altcoins. While Bitcoin remains the flagship cryptocurrency, a plethora of alternative coins—altcoins—have emerged, each with unique features, technological innovations, and visions for disrupting various industries. As the market continues to mature, investors and enthusiasts alike are watching on emerging altcoins that exhibit promise and potential to revolutionize how we interact with technology, finance, and beyond. In this section, we cast a spotlight on some of these emerging altcoins, delving into their distinct characteristics and the reasons behind their growing traction.

Solana, introduced in 2020, has garnered attention for its emphasis on scalability and speed. Built on a unique proof-of-history consensus mechanism, Solana aims to overcome the scalability challenges some of its predecessors face. Its blockchain can process many transactions per second, making it suitable for decentralized applications (DApps) that require real-time interactions. Solana's focus on performance and its compatibility with Ethereum's smart contracts have positioned it as a potential solution to the scalability concerns that often plague blockchain networks.

Polygon, formerly known as Matic Network, is dedicated to improving Ethereum's scalability and user experience. By providing a framework for creating Ethereum-compatible blockchains, Polygon aims to alleviate congestion on the Ethereum network and enable faster, cheaper transactions. Its layer 2 solution facilitates the creation of sidechains, allowing developers to build decentralized applications that benefit from Ethereum's security while enjoying enhanced scalability.

The 2020 release of Avalanche promises to provide a platform that allow developers to build unique blockchain networks that are tailored to particular use cases. Avalanche's consensus mechanism focuses on achieving both decentralization and high throughput. By offering interoperability between different blockchain networks, Avalanche seeks to foster a collaborative ecosystem where projects can leverage each other's strengths to deliver innovative solutions.

Terra, founded in 2018, focuses on bridging the gap between cryptocurrencies and stablecoins. Its stablecoin, TerraUSD (UST), is designed to maintain price stability by algorithmically adjusting its supply. Terra leverages a combination of stablecoin stability and blockchain technology to facilitate cross-border transactions, remittances, and everyday commerce, aiming to disrupt traditional financial systems while minimizing the volatility often associated with cryptocurrencies.

Chia, introduced by Bram Cohen, the creator of BitTorrent, seeks to address concerns about the environmental impact of cryptocurrency mining. Chia introduces a new consensus mechanism called "proof of space and time," where participants use their unused hard drive space instead of energy-intensive computational power to validate transactions. Chia's approach aligns with growing calls for more sustainable blockchain technologies.

Axie Infinity, although not a traditional altcoin, is a blockchain-based game that has garnered significant attention for its innovative utilization of non-fungible tokens (NFTs). Players collect and battle creatures called Axies, which are represented as NFTs. These NFTs can be bought, sold, and traded on blockchain marketplaces, creating a virtual economy within the game. Axie Infinity's success highlights the potential for blockchain technology to disrupt the gaming industry.

The emergence of these altcoins reflects the dynamic nature of the cryptocurrency landscape, where innovation and experimentation lead to the birth of diverse projects with unique value propositions. However, it's important to note that the world of cryptocurrencies is characterized by volatility and risk. Investing in emerging altcoins requires thorough research, a deep understanding of the technology, and a clear recognition of the potential rewards and pitfalls.

In conclusion, emerging altcoins are a testament to the continuous evolution of the cryptocurrency space. From addressing scalability challenges to pioneering sustainable solutions and reimagining industries like gaming, these altcoins hold the potential to reshape how we interact with technology and financial systems. While the path forward may be marked by uncertainty and hurdles, these emerging altcoins shine a light on the boundless possibilities that lie ahead—a landscape where innovation, disruption, and transformation converge to redefine the future.

Evaluating ICOs, STOs, and IEOs

The rise of cryptocurrencies as well as blockchain technology has ushered in a new era of fundraising through token offerings. Initial Coin Offerings (ICOs), Security Token Offerings (STOs), and Initial Exchange Offerings (IEOs) have become prominent ways for projects to raise capital, democratize investment, and fund innovative ventures. However, as with any investment opportunity, navigating the world of token offerings requires careful evaluation, understanding the nuances of each offering type, and assessing potential risks and rewards. In this section, we delve into the intricacies of evaluating ICOs, STOs, and IEOs, shedding light on the factors to consider when assessing these investment opportunities.

Initial Coin Offerings (ICOs) marked the initial foray into the world of token offerings. In an ICO, projects issue utility tokens to raise funds for development. These tokens often provide access to the project's ecosystem, products, or services. When evaluating an ICO, it's crucial to examine the project's whitepaper—a document outlining its goals, technology, and roadmap. Scrutinize the team's expertise, assess the viability of the project's use case, and determine whether the project solves a real-world problem. Investigate the token's utility within the ecosystem and evaluate the market demand for the project's offering. However, ICOs gained notoriety for fraudulent projects and regulatory concerns, emphasizing the importance of thorough due diligence and skepticism.

Security Token Offerings (STOs) represent a convergence of traditional finance and blockchain technology. Unlike utility tokens, security tokens derive their value from external assets or financial instruments, such as equity, debt, or real estate. STOs provide a level of regulatory compliance and investor protection that is absent in many ICOs. When evaluating STOs, analyze the project's legal structure, the assets backing the security tokens, and the level of transparency provided to investors. Assess the regulatory environment in the project's jurisdiction and verify whether the offering adheres to securities regulations. While STOs offer a bridge to more regulated investment opportunities, they may also have liquidity and market access limitations.

Initial Exchange Offerings (IEOs) emerged as a response to the challenges faced by ICOs in terms of fraud and regulatory uncertainty. In an IEO, a cryptocurrency exchange facilitates the token sale on behalf of the project. This process streamlines fundraising and leverages the exchange's user base and reputation. When evaluating an IEO, research the exchange hosting the offering—assess its credibility, security measures, and history of successful projects. Scrutinize the project's fundamentals, team, and whitepaper as you would with an ICO. Additionally, understand the terms of the IEO, including the allocation of tokens, vesting periods, and lock-up agreements. While IEOs provide a layer of legitimacy, reliance on a single exchange introduces its own set of risks.

Several factors should guide your decision-making process when evaluating ICOs, STOs, and IEOs. Begin by researching the project's team—evaluate their expertise, track record, and credibility. Scrutinize the project's whitepaper to understand its goals, technology, and implementation plan. Assess the market demand for the project's offering and its potential for adoption. Additionally, delve into the project's regulatory compliance—understand the legal framework in the project's jurisdiction and verify that the offering adheres to relevant regulations. Analyze the tokenomics— understand the token's utility, distribution, and potential for value appreciation.

To mitigate risks associated with token offerings, consider diversifying your investments across different projects and offerings. Be cautious of projects that promise guaranteed returns or appear too good to be true. Engage with the crypto community and seek insights from experts and reputable sources. Conduct thorough due diligence, verify information independently, and stay informed about regulatory developments that could impact your investment.

In conclusion, evaluating ICOs, STOs, and IEOs requires a balanced approach of scrutiny, research, and skepticism. While these token offerings offer opportunities for funding innovative projects and democratizing investment, they also carry risks related to regulatory compliance, fraudulent projects, and market volatility. By understanding the nuances of each offering type, assessing the project's fundamentals, and mitigating risks through diligent research, investors can navigate the evolving landscape of token offerings with greater confidence and informed decision-making.

CHAPTER VIII

Long-Term vs. Short-Term Investments

Exploring Long-Term HODLing Strategies

In the ever-evolving landscape of cryptocurrencies, the concept of "HODLing" has become a steadfast philosophy for many investors. Coined from a typo-turned-meme in a Bitcoin forum, "HODL" reflects the idea of holding onto your digital assets through market fluctuations and price volatility. While some investors are drawn to the fast- paced world of trading and speculation, long-term HODLing strategies offer an alternative approach—a patient and strategic stance that seeks to capitalize on the transformative potential of cryptocurrencies over extended periods. In this section, we delve into the nuances of long-term HODLing strategies, uncovering the principles, benefits, and considerations that guide this investment approach.

At the heart of the long-term HODLing philosophy lies patience—a willingness to weather market ups and downs without succumbing to impulsive decisions driven by short-term volatility. This strategy is supported by the idea that blockchain technology has the capacity to completely alter industries, financial institutions, and social standards. HODLers demonstrate a conviction in the long-term viability of cryptocurrencies, recognizing that market fluctuations are inherent to any emerging asset class.

In long-term HODLing, the focus shifts from short-term price movements to fundamental analysis—assessing a cryptocurrency's intrinsic value, technology, and utility. Investors evaluate factors such as the project's team, technology, use case, and adoption potential. By selecting assets with strong fundamentals, HODLers aim to position themselves for success over the long haul. In order to discover projects that are in line with long-term objectives, research and due diligence are essential.

While long-term HODLing strategies emphasize patience, diversification remains a key consideration. Spreading investments across different cryptocurrencies reduces the impact of a single project's underperformance. The crypto market is dynamic, with projects continuously evolving and emerging. Diversification helps mitigate risk and captures potential upside from multiple sources while recognizing that not all projects will succeed in the long run.

Long-term HODLing doesn't equate to complacency. Investors need to stay informed about developments in the cryptocurrency space, regulatory changes, and shifts in market dynamics. Regularly reassessing the fundamentals of the chosen assets is crucial. While the goal is to hold through market fluctuations, periodic adjustments based on changing circumstances can contribute to a more resilient strategy.

Long-term HODLing capitalizes on the power of compounding—allowing your investments to grow over time. By reinvesting gains and letting your portfolio appreciate, the effects of compounding can be substantial over the years. This approach leverages time as an ally, enabling gradual accumulation and potential wealth creation.

Markets for cryptocurrencies are notorious for their high volatility, which can cause feelings of fear and greed. Long-term HODLers seek to overcome these emotional rollercoasters by embracing a steadier mindset. This philosophy urges investors to keep an eye on the bigger picture and potential impact of the technology rather than acting hastily based on short-term price fluctuations.

Long-term HODLing isn't just a financial strategy—it's a psychological and emotional one as well. Staying committed to your investments through market downturns and periods of uncertainty can be challenging. The ability to remain resilient, patient, and confident in the face of adversity is a hallmark of successful long-term HODLers.

Long-term HODLing strategies offer several benefits. They simplify investment decisions, reducing the need for constant monitoring and trading. This approach aligns with the "buy and hold" philosophy that has proven successful in traditional investing. Long-term HODLers often avoid the stress associated with frequent trading and market timing. Moreover, investors may benefit from potential bull runs that bring substantial returns by holding through market cycles.

However, long-term HODLing has its considerations. While patience is a virtue, it's important to periodically reassess your portfolio and adjust your strategy based on new information. Cryptocurrency markets are still maturing, and while some projects hold promise, others may fail to deliver on their potential. The landscape may be impacted by legislative modifications, advancements in technology, and changes in market sentiment.

In conclusion, long-term HODLing strategies in cryptocurrency offer an alternative approach to trading and speculation. Rooted in patience, conviction, and fundamental analysis, this strategy embraces the transformative potential of blockchain technology. While it demands a steadfast commitment and a strong emotional foundation, long-term HODLing leverages time, compounding, and a focus on fundamentals to position investors for the potential rewards that can come from patiently weathering market fluctuations. As the cryptocurrency ecosystem continues to evolve, long-term HODLing is a testament to the power of strategic patience in an ever-changing digital landscape.

Pros and Cons of Short-Term Trading

Cryptocurrency investment has evolved beyond its original purpose of digital cash, giving rise to many strategies tailored to various risk profiles and investment goals. Among these strategies, short-term trading has gained prominence as a way to capitalize on the volatility of the crypto market. Short-term traders, often called "day traders" or "swing traders," aim to profit from rapid price fluctuations within short timeframes. While short- term trading offers the allure of quick gains, it also comes with its own set of challenges and risks.

The primary allure of short-term trading is the potential for quick gains. The extraordinary volatility of the cryptocurrency markets gives traders an opportunity to profit from price changes that occur within minutes, hours, or days. Cryptocurrency markets operate 24/7, allowing short-term traders to enter and exit positions conveniently. This liquidity and accessibility facilitate the execution of trades and the ability to react swiftly to market developments. Additionally, short-term trading often relies heavily on technical analysis—studying price charts, patterns, and indicators to predict short-term movements. Skilled technical analysts can identify trends, entry and exit points, and potential reversals.

Cryptocurrency markets offer a wide range of trading instruments, including spot trading, margin trading, and derivatives like futures and options. This variety allows traders to tailor their strategies to different risk levels and market conditions. Moreover, while long-term investments may suffer during prolonged market downturns, skilled short-term traders can profit from both upward and downward price movements, capitalizing on volatility regardless of market direction.

However, short-term trading has its drawbacks. It inherently carries a high risk level due to the crypto market's rapid price fluctuations. The pressure to make split-second decisions and constantly monitor price movements can be mentally and emotionally taxing. Moreover, successful short-term trading demands a deep understanding of technical analysis, chart patterns, and market indicators. Novice traders may find it challenging to make profitable decisions consistently. Transaction fees can also pose a challenge, as frequent trading can lead to substantial costs that eat into profits. Additionally, cryptocurrency markets are susceptible to market manipulation by large players and "whales" who can trigger price movements to their advantage. This unpredictability can lead to unexpected losses for traders.

Furthermore, short-term trading exposes traders to psychological pressures such as fear, greed, and FOMO (fear of missing out). Emotional decision-making can lead to impulsive trades and losses. While short-term trading offers potential gains, weighing the pros and cons before adopting this strategy is essential. Successful short-term trading requires a combination of technical expertise, emotional discipline, risk management, and a thorough understanding of the market's dynamics. Traders considering this approach should invest time in learning about technical analysis, practice strict risk management, and develop a well-defined trading plan. Investing in short-term trading should be informed, measured, and aligned with one's risk tolerance and investment goals.

Day Trading, Swing Trading, and Scalping

Different trading strategies have emerged to cater to various risk appetites and market conditions in the fast-paced world of cryptocurrency investment. Among these strategies, day trading, swing trading, and scalping are popular approaches that capitalize on price movements within different timeframes. These strategies offer distinct advantages and challenges, appealing to traders seeking quick profits, short-term gains, and precise execution.

Day trading is a high-intensity strategy where traders buy and sell cryptocurrencies within a single trading day. The objective is to execute a number of trades throughout the day in an attempt to profit from short-term price movements. Day traders typically rely on technical analysis, studying price charts, patterns, and indicators to identify potential entry and exit points. They seek to profit from intraday trends, often leveraging margin trading to amplify gains (and losses). Day trading requires constant vigilance, as positions are closed before the trading day ends to avoid overnight risks.

Day trading offers an opportunity to make quick profits because intraday volatility can cause sharp price changes. Moreover, day traders are not exposed to overnight market risks, such as news events that could impact prices while markets are closed. However, day trading requires high technical expertise, emotional discipline, and the ability to make split-second decisions. The pressure to monitor markets consistently and execute timely trades can be mentally and emotionally taxing. Additionally, transaction fees can accumulate due to the frequent trading activity, impacting overall profitability.

Swing trading involves capturing price movements over a few days to a few weeks, aiming to profit from short- to medium-term trends. Swing traders analyze both technical and fundamental factors, seeking assets with potential catalysts that could drive price movements. This strategy requires a balance between the patience to hold positions through short-term volatility and the agility to exit when the trend reverses. Swing traders often use stop-loss and take-profit orders to manage risk and secure gains.

The advantages of swing trading include the potential for larger gains compared to day trading, as swing traders aim to capture the momentum of multi-day trends. This approach also allows for a more relaxed trading schedule, as traders don't need to monitor markets as intensely as day traders. Swing traders can combine their trading activities with other commitments, making it suitable for those with limited time. However, swing trading still demands a strong grasp of technical analysis and market dynamics. Timing entries and exits accurately is essential to capitalize on trend movements.

Scalping is a technique focused on profiting from small price movements over a very short timeframe, often within minutes or seconds. Scalpers execute a large volume of trades to capture small gains from each trade. This strategy requires precision in timing and execution and low latency trading platforms to take advantage of fleeting opportunities. Scalpers often target assets with high liquidity to ensure smooth execution of trades.

The main advantage of scalping is the potential for consistent, although small, gains due to the high trading frequency. Scalpers are not heavily exposed to overnight risks, as positions are typically closed before the trading day ends. However, scalping demands a substantial amount of time, focus, and quick decision-making. The pressure to execute trades swiftly can lead to stress and emotional fatigue. Scalping is also sensitive to transaction costs, as frequent trading can result in substantial fees that erode profits.

Selecting the right trading strategy depends on factors such as risk tolerance, time availability, technical expertise, and market conditions. Day trading offers quick profits but requires constant monitoring and quick decision-making. Swing trading allows for larger gains over a short- to medium-term horizon and offers a more relaxed trading schedule. Scalping offers consistent gains from micro-movements but demands intense focus and execution speed.

In the multifaceted realm of cryptocurrency investing, where strategies vary and trends evolve, there are foundational principles that transcend individual approaches. These principles serve as guiding lights, directing investors toward success regardless of their chosen path. As you navigate the intricate landscape of crypto investments, consider these essential principles that underpin effective and prudent decision-making.

A comprehensive education is paramount whether you're pursuing day trading, HODLing, or any other strategy. Develop a deep understanding of technical analysis, recognizing chart patterns, market indicators, and the dynamics that drive price movements. A well-informed investor is better equipped to make rational decisions, utilizing data-driven insights to guide their strategy.

Risk is inherent in any investment endeavor, but effective risk management is the cornerstone of responsible investing. Implement risk management tools like stop- loss and take-profit orders to protect your capital and mitigate potential losses. By defining your risk tolerance and setting limits on both gains and losses, you maintain control over your investments even in volatile markets.

The crypto space is notorious for its volatility, capable of evoking intense emotions in investors. Embracing emotional discipline is essential for maintaining a steady course amidst market fluctuations. Regardless of your strategy, adhering to your pre-defined plan and resisting the pull of emotions can prevent impulsive decisions that might undermine your long-term goals.

Cryptocurrency markets are dynamic and subject to swift changes. Staying informed about market developments, regulatory shifts, and technological advancements is key to remaining adaptable. A successful investor is one who can adjust their strategy when conditions evolve. This adaptability allows you to align your approach with the prevailing market dynamics, optimizing your chances of success.

Before committing substantial capital to any strategy, practice is an invaluable step. Simulation environments, often offered by trading platforms, allow you to execute trades without real financial risk. This practice hones your decision-making skills, familiarizes you with the nuances of your chosen strategy, and builds the confidence needed for live trading.

In conclusion, day trading, swing trading, and scalping offer distinct approaches to cryptocurrency investment, each with its own set of benefits and challenges. These strategies cater to different trader preferences, risk profiles, and market conditions. Successful execution requires a combination of technical expertise, emotional discipline, risk management, and a deep understanding of market dynamics. Traders should carefully evaluate their goals and capabilities before adopting a particular strategy, recognizing that there is no one-size-fits-all approach in the ever-changing world of cryptocurrency trading.

CHAPTER IX

Market Sentiment and News Analysis

Understanding the Role of News and Sentiment

In the dynamic realm of cryptocurrency investment, where markets operate 24/7 and volatility is the norm, the role of news and sentiment cannot be underestimated. Unlike traditional financial markets, the cryptocurrency ecosystem is still relatively young and highly influenced by news events, media coverage, and the collective sentiment of participants. Making educated decisions and managing the complexities of this fast- changing environment require an understanding of how news and sentiment affect cryptocurrency investment.

News has a profound impact on cryptocurrency markets. Positive news can lead to rapid price surges, while negative news can trigger sharp declines. This is due in part to the nascent nature of the cryptocurrency industry. Unlike established markets, where fundamentals often drive price movements, news flow and market sentiment heavily influence the crypto market. Major developments, such as regulatory announcements, technological breakthroughs, partnerships, and adoption by large corporations, can send ripples through the market, sparking both excitement and apprehension.

For instance, news of a government embracing blockchain technology can lead to optimism about future adoption and growth, causing prices to rise. Conversely, news of a security breach at a cryptocurrency exchange can erode investor confidence and lead to a sell-off. Traders and investors keenly monitor news outlets, social media platforms, and forums for timely updates that can impact their positions. News can create short-term trading opportunities and also shape long-term investment strategies.

Sentiment, often driven by news, is pivotal in shaping market dynamics. The crypto market is highly sensitive to shifts in investor sentiment—fear, greed, optimism, and skepticism. Social media sites including Twitter, Reddit, and Telegram have developed into virtual forums for the expression of thoughts and the amplifaction of sentiment. Cryptocurrency projects often have dedicated communities that contribute to shaping market perception.

FOMO (fear of missing out) and also FUD (fear, uncertainty, and doubt) are common terms in crypto, highlighting the emotional undercurrents that can drive market movements. Positive sentiment can lead to frenzied buying and price spikes, fueled by a sense of opportunity and the fear of missing out on potential gains. Conversely, negative sentiment can trigger panic selling and sharp price drops, driven by concerns and doubts about the future.

The volatile nature of sentiment-driven price swings poses both opportunities and risks. Investors who understand how sentiment shapes the market can capitalize on short-term trends. However, sentiment-driven movements can also lead to market overreactions, creating a fertile ground for manipulation and unsustainable price bubbles.

While news and sentiment provide valuable insights, analyzing and interpreting them effectively can be challenging. The cryptocurrency landscape is rife with misinformation, rumors, and unverified reports that can significantly impact sentiment. Traders and investors must exercise caution and verify information from credible sources before making decisions based on news.

Various tools and platforms have emerged to gauge sentiment and provide sentiment analysis to navigate these challenges. Natural language processing (NLP) algorithms are used to scan news articles, social media posts, and forum discussions to assess the prevailing sentiment. These tools assign sentiment scores, categorizing content as positive, negative, or neutral. While not foolproof, sentiment analysis can provide a broader perspective on market sentiment beyond individual biases and emotions.

Effective cryptocurrency investment requires striking a delicate balance between fundamental analysis and sentiment analysis. While news and sentiment play a significant role in short-term price movements, long-term success hinges on solid fundamentals. Projects with robust technology, adoption potential, and a skilled development team are more likely to weather short-term fluctuations driven by sentiment.

Investors in the cryptocurrency space must adopt a multidimensional approach to navigate the complex and often volatile market. One fundamental aspect is sourcing information from diversified sources. Relying on multiple reputable news outlets and industry experts helps verify information and minimize the risk of being misled by misinformation, which is particularly prevalent in the digital age.

Critical thinking is another crucial skill that investors should hone. Not all news events have the same impact, and emotions and market psychology can influence the sentiment surrounding them. Careful consideration of the context, potential biases, and the credibility of the news source is essential to make well-informed decisions.

While short-term sentiment-driven trades can yield profits, long-term success requires a broader perspective. A project's core fundamentals and adoption potential may not be aligned with judgments made in haste while only considering short-term sentiment fluctuations. Taking a long-term view allows investors to assess the viability and sustainability of a cryptocurrency project beyond the immediate market sentiment.

Leveraging sentiment analysis tools can provide valuable insights into the broader sentiment prevailing in the market. These tools, powered by data analytics and natural language processing, help gauge the overall mood and sentiment of the cryptocurrency community. While not infallible, such tools can help investors identify trends and potential shifts in market sentiment, contributing to a more comprehensive investment strategy.

Effective risk management is crucial in any investment endeavor, including crypto. Despite its influence, sentiment can be volatile and driven by emotional impulses. Managing risk involves setting clear investment goals, determining acceptable levels of loss, and sticking to a well-defined strategy, regardless of market sentiment. Embracing a disciplined approach helps prevent emotional decision-making that can lead to losses.

In the intricate world of cryptocurrency investment, news and sentiment share a symbiotic relationship. News events fuel sentiment, and sentiment, in turn, shapes market reactions. Recognizing the interplay between these factors is essential for investors seeking to navigate the volatile cryptocurrency landscape. While news and sentiment-driven trading can be lucrative, a foundation of solid research, risk management, and a long-term perspective remains crucial for building a successful cryptocurrency investment strategy. As the industry evolves, news and sentiment will remain influential forces that demand vigilance and a discerning approach from investors and traders alike.

Evaluating Reliable Crypto News Sources

In cryptocurrency's dynamic and rapidly evolving landscape, staying informed is not just an advantage, but a necessity. The crypto market operates 24/7 and is known for its extreme volatility. As a result, news and information play a crucial role in influencing market sentiment and driving price movements. However, navigating the world of crypto news can be a challenge, as the sheer volume of sources, varying degrees of reliability, and the ever-present threat of misinformation can make it difficult to separate fact from fiction. Therefore, the ability to evaluate and choose reliable crypto news sources is a skill that every investor in the crypto space must develop.

The landscape of crypto news sources is diverse, ranging from traditional financial media outlets that cover cryptocurrencies as part of their broader coverage, to specialized crypto news websites, forums, social media platforms, and influential figures within the crypto community. Unlike traditional financial markets, where established and recognized media outlets are often considered trustworthy sources, the crypto market lacks a universally accepted authority. As a result, a multitude of sources exist, each with its own level of credibility and authenticity. This democratization of information sharing is powerful, but it also creates concerns with accuracy and dependability.

Misinformation is a significant concern in the crypto news space. The fast-paced nature of digital communication allows both accurate information and fake news to spread quickly. The decentralized nature of the crypto industry itself creates an environment where false narratives and sensationalism can thrive. False reports about regulatory changes, technological breakthroughs, or market trends can trigger rapid and drastic price fluctuations, leading to financial losses for those who act on unreliable information. In this context, the importance of evaluating the credibility of news sources becomes even more pronounced.

The criteria for evaluating reliable crypto news sources encompass several essential factors. First and foremost is the credibility and reputation of the news source. Established media outlets with a history of accurate and responsible reporting are generally considered more reliable. Reputable news organizations adhere to rigorous fact-checking procedures and ethical journalistic standards. Investigating the background and expertise of the authors or reporters is also crucial. Authors experienced in cryptocurrency and with a track record of producing well-informed and accurate content are more likely to provide reliable insights.

Another important criterion is the editorial standards of the news outlet. Trusted sources follow strict editorial guidelines, ensuring accuracy, transparency, and accountability in their reporting. Verifiable sources and citations within the news articles are another indicator of reliability. Credible articles should provide references that support the claims being made. Cross-referencing information from multiple sources is also essential. If a piece of news is only reported by one outlet and not corroborated by others, it should be treated with caution until verified.

Bias and objectivity are considerations that cannot be overlooked. While bias is inherent to human communication, a balanced news source strives to present multiple perspectives on a topic. Evaluating the potential bias of a news outlet helps in understanding its underlying agenda and motivations. Furthermore, the consistency and accuracy of a news outlet's reporting history are crucial factors. Frequent errors, retractions, or sensationalism can indicate a lack of credibility.

In the digital age, the spread of news extends beyond traditional media outlets to social media platforms and online forums. While these platforms can provide real-time updates and insights, they are also breeding grounds for rumors and misinformation. Engaging in productive discussions and seeking out well-reasoned analysis from reputable individuals can enhance one's understanding of market trends and sentiment. However, due diligence is required to ensure that the information being consumed is accurate and well-sourced.

Cultivating a critical mindset is a key aspect of evaluating crypto news sources. While reliable sources provide valuable insights, no source is infallible. Investors should approach news with skepticism and verify information before making investment decisions. Developing a network of trusted sources and experts can provide a more comprehensive perspective on the market. Additionally, paying attention to the track record of news outlets and observing how they respond to mistakes or corrections can provide insight into their commitment to accuracy and transparency.

In conclusion, evaluating reliable crypto news sources is a critical skill for investors and enthusiasts in the cryptocurrency space. The decentralized and fast-paced nature of the industry has led to a plethora of news sources, each with varying levels of credibility. Making informed investment decisions and navigating the constantly evolving crypto market require the ability to differentiate credible sources from unreliable ones. By applying a set of evaluation criteria, staying informed through trusted outlets, and maintaining a critical mindset, investors can navigate the challenges of misinformation and make more well-informed choices in their crypto journey. As the cryptocurrency industry continues to evolve, the importance of reliable news sources will only grow, making this skill more valuable than ever.

Making Informed Decisions Amid Market Volatility

The cryptocurrency market, characterized by its inherent volatility, offers both substantial opportunities and significant risks to investors. Rapid price fluctuations are a hallmark of this dynamic ecosystem, driven by a range of factors including news events, market sentiment, regulatory developments, technological advancements, and macroeconomic trends. Navigating such volatility requires a thoughtful and informed approach that encompasses a deep understanding of the market, solid risk management strategies, and the ability to make rational decisions amidst emotional turbulence.

Volatility is an integral part of the cryptocurrency market. Prices of cryptocurrencies can swing dramatically within short timeframes, often defying traditional market norms. There are a number of reasons specific to the cryptocurrency ecosystem that cause this volatility.

Regulatory uncertainty, lack of established valuation models, relatively small market capitalization compared to traditional assets, and a speculative nature contribute to the heightened price swings observed in the crypto market.

While volatility can be daunting for investors, it is also what makes the cryptocurrency market alluring. The potential for substantial gains within a short period can be enticing, but it comes with an equally significant risk of losses. As a result, effective strategies to navigate volatility are imperative for those looking to engage in cryptocurrency investment.

Amid market volatility, fundamental analysis emerges as a pillar of stability. Unlike short-term price fluctuations driven by sentiment, fundamentals encompass a cryptocurrency project's intrinsic value and long-term viability. Factors such as the project's technology, use case, adoption potential, development team, and market demand contribute to its fundamentals.

By conducting thorough fundamental analysis, investors can identify projects with strong underlying foundations that are more likely to weather market volatility. Focusing on long-term viability rather than short-term price fluctuations helps to mitigate the risks associated with volatile market conditions. However, it's important to note that even fundamentally strong projects are not immune to short-term price swings, given the influence of external factors.

Technical analysis is another tool at the disposal of cryptocurrency investors seeking to navigate market volatility. This approach involves studying historical price data and chart patterns to identify trends, support and resistance levels, and potential entry and exit points.

While technical analysis is primarily used for short- to medium-term trading, it can provide valuable insights to help investors time their entries and exits more effectively.

Investors can benefit from short-term market changes while minimizing volatility risk by incorporating technical analysis into their investment plans. However, it's crucial to approach technical analysis with caution and not rely solely on it, as the cryptocurrency market can sometimes defy traditional technical patterns due to its unique dynamics.

Risk management is a cornerstone of successful investment strategies, particularly in a volatile market like cryptocurrencies. Adopting a disciplined approach to risk involves setting clear investment goals, determining acceptable levels of loss, and diversifying one's portfolio. Diversification across different cryptocurrencies and asset classes can mitigate the impact of sudden price drops on a single investment.

Setting stop-loss orders, which automatically trigger a sell order if a cryptocurrency's price drops to a specified level, is a common risk management technique. While stop-loss orders can protect capital, they should be set strategically to avoid triggering a sale during normal price fluctuations. Take-profit orders, which automatically trigger a sell order when a certain price target is reached, can also help lock in profits during periods of price volatility.

Market volatility not only tests investment strategies but also challenges the emotional resilience of investors. Emotional reactions, such as panic selling during price drops or FOMO-driven buying during price surges, can lead to suboptimal decisions. Developing emotional discipline is crucial in a volatile market, where fear and greed can cloud rational judgment.

Investors should set clear investment objectives and stick to a well-defined strategy even when market sentiment is tumultuous. Seeking advice from trusted sources and maintaining a long-term perspective can help counteract emotional impulses. Surrounding oneself with a supportive community of fellow investors and staying informed about market developments can contribute to making more rational decisions amid market turbulence.

The cryptocurrency market is always changing, so staying educated is essential for making wise choices in an unstable environment. Engaging in continuous learning about the market, new projects, technological advancements, and regulatory changes equips investors with the knowledge needed to adapt to shifting market conditions.

Reading research reports, attending webinars and conferences, taking part in online communities, and using dependable information sources can all help you gain insightful knowledge and a deeper comprehension of the market environment. A knowledgeable investor is better able to distinguish real possibilities from passing the hype and to make choices that fit their tolerance for risk and investing objectives.

The cryptocurrency market's inherent volatility is a double-edged sword: it presents lucrative gains opportunities and exposes investors to substantial risks. Making informed decisions amid market volatility requires a holistic approach that encompasses fundamental and technical analysis, risk management, emotional discipline, and continuous education. By understanding the nature of market volatility, conducting thorough research, adopting disciplined risk management strategies, and cultivating emotional resilience, investors can navigate the choppy waters of the cryptocurrency market with greater confidence and effectiveness. As the market continues to evolve, adapting and making rational decisions in the face of volatility remains a vital skill for successful cryptocurrency investors.

Avoiding Emotional Investing

The cryptocurrency market, known for its extreme volatility and rapid price fluctuations, often stirs powerful emotions among investors. Fear, greed, excitement, and panic can drive decisions that may not align with rational investment strategies. Emotional investing, driven by impulsive reactions to market movements, can lead to substantial losses and hinder long-term financial goals. As such, mastering the art of avoiding emotional investing is crucial for anyone seeking success in cryptocurrency.

The phenomena of emotional investing happens when investors make choices based on their emotions rather than a logical understanding of market trends, fundamentals, and risk concerns. The roller-coaster nature of the cryptocurrency market—where prices can skyrocket and plummet within hours—amplifies emotional responses. FOMO (fear of missing out) drives investors to buy during rallies without careful consideration, while FUD (fear, uncertainty, and doubt) prompts panic selling during market dips.

One of the most significant challenges of emotional investing is that it often leads to reactive decision-making. Investors caught in the heat of the moment may disregard sound investment principles and succumb to irrational actions driven by psychological factors.

Emotional investing can quickly erode profits, undermine long-term strategies, and contribute to a cycle of loss-making trades.

A rational approach to investing involves making decisions based on a thorough analysis of data, facts, and well-defined investment goals. This approach requires discipline, patience, and the ability to detach from emotional impulses when making investment decisions. A few key strategies can help investors steer clear of emotional investing.

Clear investment objectives and a well-defined strategy serve as an anchor against emotional reactions. Rational investors know their risk tolerance, time horizon, and desired outcomes, allowing them to resist the urge to chase short-term gains.

Conducting thorough research before investing is a fundamental aspect of rational decision-making. Investigating a cryptocurrency project's fundamentals, technology, adoption potential, and development team provides a solid foundation for informed choices.

Implementing risk management strategies, like setting stop-loss and take-profit orders, helps limit potential losses and prevent panic selling during price downturns. Diversification across different assets also reduces the impact of a single investment's poor performance.

Continuous learning about the cryptocurrency market, technology advancements, regulatory changes, and industry trends builds a comprehensive understanding. Informed investors are more likely to make rational decisions based on knowledge rather than emotion.

Cryptocurrency investments should be approached with a long-term perspective. Market volatility is often short- lived, and focusing on long-term growth potential helps investors ride out short-term price fluctuations.

Emotional investing can be exacerbated by the herd mentality, where investors follow the crowd's actions without critical analysis. Relying on independent research and analysis helps counteract the influence of the herd. Understanding that market downturns are a natural part of investing prepares rational investors for such scenarios. Instead of reacting with panic, they can assess the situation calmly and make decisions aligned with their strategy.

Recognizing and controlling the emotions of fear and greed is crucial. Avoiding impulsive decisions driven by FOMO during price rallies and resisting the urge to sell due to FUD during market dips are essential aspects of rational investing.

A rational approach to investing requires cultivating a disciplined mindset and understanding the psychological biases that can lead to emotional investing. Investors who experience loss aversion, in which the pain of losses is more profound than the pleasure of wins, can make irrational choices. Overconfidence bias may lead investors to believe they can accurately predict market movements, resulting in risky trades.

Investors should acknowledge that emotions are a natural part of investing but must be managed to avoid impulsive actions. Self-awareness, mindfulness, and developing a strong sense of emotional discipline can aid in maintaining a rational perspective during turbulent market conditions.

In the fast-paced and emotionally charged world of cryptocurrency investing, the ability to avoid emotional decision-making is a distinguishing factor between successful and unsuccessful investors. Mastering the art of rational investing involves a combination of clear goals, diligent research, risk management, continuous learning, and psychological awareness. Investors can navigate the volatile cryptocurrency landscape with resilience and confidence by approaching investments with a long-term perspective, embracing disciplined strategies, and resisting the allure of short-term emotional reactions. In an environment where emotions often run high, the rational investor stands out as a beacon of level-headedness and foresight, securing their financial future amid the waves of market turbulence.

CHAPTER X

Case Studies: Learning from Successful Investors

Real-Life Success Stories in Crypto Investing

The world of cryptocurrency investing has produced both tales of incredible success and cautionary tales of loss. The stories of individuals who have achieved remarkable gains in the cryptocurrency market have captured the imagination of investors worldwide. These success stories highlight the transformative potential of cryptocurrencies and underscore the importance of strategic decision- making, risk management, and seizing opportunities in a dynamic and rapidly evolving market.

The first real-life success stories in the realm of cryptocurrency revolve around the pioneers who recognized the potential of Bitcoin when it was in its infancy. One of the most famous examples is that of Laszlo Hanyecz, who made history by completing the first recorded real-world transaction using Bitcoin. In 2010, he famously exchanged 10,000 BTC for two pizzas, marking the first tangible value attributed to the cryptocurrency. Little did he know that those Bitcoins would become worth millions of dollars in the years to come.

Another early success story is that of the Winklevoss twins, who are renowned for their involvement in the founding of Facebook. They ventured into the world of cryptocurrencies early on and reportedly invested a substantial amount of their settlement from the Facebook dispute into Bitcoin. Their foresight paid off as the value of Bitcoin surged, and they became among the first Bitcoin billionaires.

Ethereum, with its smart contract capabilities, introduced a new dimension to the cryptocurrency landscape. Vitalik Buterin, the creator of Ethereum, envisioned a decentralized platform that could facilitate complex applications beyond mere digital currency. Buterin's brainchild revolutionized blockchain technology and paved the way for a new wave of success stories.

One such story is that of the decentralized application (dApp) CryptoKitties. Launched on the Ethereum blockchain, CryptoKitties allows users to buy, sell, and breed virtual cats using Ether. The game's popularity led to a surge in Ethereum network activity and highlighted the potential of blockchain technology for novel applications beyond financial transactions.

The initial coin offering (ICO) boom of 2017 saw numerous projects raise millions of dollars in a short period. Some investors capitalized on this trend, achieving substantial returns on their investments. One such example is that of the project Ripple, which raised funds through an early-stage token sale. Those who invested early and held onto their XRP tokens saw significant returns as the project gained traction and partnerships in the financial sector.

However, the ICO frenzy also gave rise to cautionary tales of projects that promised revolutionary concepts but ultimately failed to deliver. Many investors fell victim to scams and fraudulent schemes, emphasizing the importance of due diligence and thorough research before participating in any investment opportunity.

The cryptocurrency market is not solely about Bitcoin and Ethereum. Many altcoins and tokens have experienced substantial growth, offering investors diverse investment opportunities. Binance Coin (BNB), the cryptocurrency that is native to the Binance exchange, is one example of a success story. BNB's value surged as Binance established itself as a leading exchange platform, and the coin gained utility within the Binance ecosystem.

Another success story comes from the DeFi (decentralized finance) sector. Projects like Aave, Compound, and Uniswap garnered attention for their innovative solutions in the lending and trading space. Investors who identified the potential of these projects early on saw their investments multiply as DeFi gained traction and reshaped the financial landscape.

As the cryptocurrency market matured, a new wave of investors emerged who became millionaires and even billionaires through their strategic investments. Individuals like Brian Armstrong, CEO of Coinbase, and Cameron and Tyler Winklevoss continued to build their wealth as their platforms gained prominence in the industry.

A standout example is that of Changpeng Zhao, better known as CZ, the founder and CEO of Binance. Under his leadership, Binance rapidly became one of the largest and most influential cryptocurrency exchanges globally. CZ's success story reflects the potential for visionary entrepreneurs to shape the industry and amass significant wealth in the process.

Real-life success stories in crypto investing offer aspiring and experienced investors valuable lessons. These stories underscore the significance of timing, strategy, diversification, and a willingness to take calculated risks.

While tales of extraordinary gains inspire investors, it is vital to recognize that the cryptocurrency market is inherently volatile, and only some investments will yield the same level of success.

Moreover, success in the cryptocurrency market requires more than just luck. Strategic decision-making, thorough research, risk management, and an understanding of the technological and market fundamentals are essential components of achieving favorable outcomes. Successful investors often exhibit resilience, adapting to market changes and learning from their experiences.

Cryptocurrency investing has transformed ordinary individuals into millionaires and even billionaires, capturing the attention of the global financial landscape. From the early adopters of Bitcoin to the founders of innovative projects and exchanges, the success stories in crypto investing underscore the transformative power of emerging technologies and the potential for substantial financial gains.

However, these stories also emphasize the need for a cautious and informed approach to investing. There are cautionary tales of bad investments for every success story. The cryptocurrency market's volatility, regulatory uncertainties, and technological complexities require investors to conduct due diligence, manage risks, and cultivate a comprehensive understanding of the landscape.

Real-life success stories in crypto investing serve as both inspiration and education. They remind us that the cryptocurrency market is a space of opportunity, innovation, and potential rewards, but also one that demands a strategic and informed approach. As the market continues to evolve, these stories will continue to shape the narratives of the individuals who dared to explore the uncharted territories of the digital economy.

Lessons Learned from Past Bull and Bear Markets

With its cycles of exuberant bull runs followed by sobering bear markets, the cryptocurrency market has provided investors with a dynamic and often unpredictable landscape. These alternating periods of euphoria and despair have left a trail of valuable lessons for those navigating the world of crypto investing. Examining the patterns, catalysts, and outcomes of past bull and bear markets offers insight into the market dynamics and equips investors with the knowledge needed to make informed decisions and manage risks.

Surging prices, frenzied excitement, and a sense of unstoppable growth characterize bull markets in the cryptocurrency space. Newcomers to the market are frequently drawn during these times by their fear of missing out or FOMO on possibly life-changing gains. The most recognizable bull market took place in 2017, when Bitcoin hit a record-breaking high of about $20,000 and many cryptocurrencies soared to new heights.

During bull markets, lessons of caution often become overshadowed by the allure of rapid gains. New and inexperienced investors can be particularly vulnerable to impulsive decisions driven by greed and the belief that prices will continue to rise indefinitely. However, the history of bull markets teaches us that euphoria is often followed by a sobering reality check.

Bear markets follow the exuberance of bull markets, ushering in a period of prolonged price decline and market correction. The bear market that followed the 2017 bull run was a stark reminder of the market's cyclical nature. Bitcoin's price plummeted, and many altcoins experienced significant losses. These phases of contraction test investors' resolve, expose weak projects, and challenge the narratives that fueled the previous euphoria.

Bear markets offer essential humility, risk management, and long-term thinking lessons. They serve as a reality check, reminding investors that markets do not move in a straight line, and substantial profits can quickly evaporate. Investors who learned these lessons emerged stronger, having developed a more realistic perspective on the challenges and uncertainties inherent in the crypto landscape.

Past bull and bear markets underscore the tension between speculation and fundamentals. Bull markets often see speculation reach fever pitch, with prices detached from the underlying value of projects. This speculative frenzy can lead to unsustainable growth, followed by dramatic corrections in bear markets.

Bear markets, on the other hand, emphasize the importance of fundamentals. Projects with solid technology, adoption potential, and real-world use cases are more likely to weather the storm and eventually emerge stronger. Investors who base their decisions on a project's merits rather than hype are better equipped to navigate bullish and bearish phases.

The crypto market's maturity and regulatory landscape also significantly shape the lessons learned from past cycles. The 2017 bull market drew widespread attention, leading to increased scrutiny from regulators worldwide. Subsequent bear markets witnessed regulatory actions and crackdowns on fraudulent schemes, highlighting the importance of investor protection and regulatory compliance.

Market participants have learned that regulatory developments can trigger market fluctuations and impact investor sentiment. As the industry matures, a clearer understanding of regulatory dynamics becomes essential for investors to gauge their investments' potential risks and rewards.

Lessons from past market cycles emphasize the critical role of investment strategy and emotional discipline. Investors who chase short-term gains during bull markets can suffer substantial losses during subsequent bear markets. The "buy low, sell high" mantra becomes especially relevant during market downturns, where opportunities to accumulate assets at discounted prices abound.

Emotional discipline is paramount, particularly in the face of extreme price volatility. Investors who succumb to panic selling during market crashes often miss out on the subsequent recovery. Conversely, those who can detach from emotional impulses and maintain a long-term perspective are better positioned to endure market fluctuations and benefit from the eventual resurgence of the market.

The lessons learned from past bull and bear markets in crypto investing underscore the cyclical nature of the market and the need for informed, strategic, and disciplined decision-making. Bull markets offer the potential for substantial gains but also introduce the risk of euphoria-driven mistakes. Bear markets provide a reality check, fostering humility and encouraging investors to prioritize fundamentals and long-term perspectives.

Understanding the interplay between speculation and fundamentals, market maturity, regulatory impact, investment strategy, and emotional discipline equips investors to navigate the waves of the cryptocurrency landscape. These lessons serve as guideposts for novice and experienced investors, reminding us that a holistic and informed approach is essential for success in an ever-evolving market.

The lessons from past market cycles remain relevant as the cryptocurrency market continues to evolve. By heeding these lessons, investors can position themselves to weather the storms of bear markets and capitalize on the opportunities presented by bull markets. The journey through the highs and lows of crypto investing is a continuous learning experience that demands a balance of knowledge, strategy, and emotional resilience to navigate the dynamic world of digital assets.

Strategies Employed by Seasoned Investors

Seasoned investors in the realm of cryptocurrency have honed their strategies over years of navigating the dynamic and often volatile market. Their approaches reflect a blend of strategic thinking, risk management, and adaptability to the ever-changing landscape of digital assets. These experienced individuals have developed a toolkit of strategies that enable them to maximize opportunities, mitigate risks, and achieve success in a market known for its rapid fluctuations and transformative potential.

One of the foundational strategies seasoned investors employ is the long-term investment approach, often called "HODLing." This strategy involves holding onto assets over an extended period, regardless of short-term price fluctuations. Seasoned investors recognize the volatile cryptocurrency market but also acknowledge its potential for significant long-term growth. By adopting a patient outlook, they can weather market downturns and capitalize on the potential for substantial gains as the market matures.

An important investing plan principle that seasoned cryptocurrency investors follow is diversification. Rather than placing all their bets on a single asset, they allocate their investments across various cryptocurrencies. This approach helps mitigate the impact of poor-performing assets on their overall portfolio. It's a strategy that acknowledges the unpredictability of individual assets and aims to reduce risk by spreading investments across various projects with varying levels of risk and potential reward.

Experienced investors understand the importance of thorough research and due diligence. They analyze the fundamentals of each cryptocurrency project before investing, evaluating factors such as technology, use case, adoption potential, and the competence of the development team. By scrutinizing the underlying strengths and weaknesses of projects, they can make informed decisions grounded in understanding the project's viability and long-term prospects.

Technical analysis, which involves studying historical price data and patterns to predict future price movements, is another tool in the arsenal of seasoned investors. While controversial among some market participants, technical analysis provides insights into market trends and sentiment. Experienced investors combine technical analysis with fundamental analysis to make more well-rounded decisions, understanding that timing is crucial in the highly volatile crypto market.

Market sentiment can influence price movements, creating opportunities for investors who know how to read it. Seasoned investors often adopt a contrarian approach, buying when the market is pessimistic and selling when the market is euphoric. This strategy involves capitalizing on emotional market swings by recognizing that sentiment-driven price fluctuations can lead to mispriced assets.

While long-term investment is a prevalent strategy, some seasoned investors engage in active trading. Day trading, swing trading, and scalping involve more frequent buying and selling of assets to profit from short-term price movements. These strategies require a deep understanding of market dynamics, technical analysis, and risk management. Seasoned traders often leverage their experience to execute precise trades and capitalize on short-term opportunities.

Staking and yield farming are strategies that leverage decentralized finance (DeFi) protocols to earn rewards by holding and lending assets. Seasoned investors use these opportunities to generate passive income and increase their overall returns. These strategies also reflect a forward-thinking approach, as they align with the broader trend of decentralized financial services.

Experienced investors recognize the potential for significant gains by participating in early-stage opportunities, such as initial coin offerings (ICOs), security token offerings (STOs), and initial exchange offerings (IEOs). However, they cautiously approach these opportunities and conduct thorough research to identify projects with genuine potential. They know the risks associated with investing in early-stage projects and consider their investment part of a diversified portfolio.

In the rapidly evolving cryptocurrency landscape, seasoned investors understand the importance of adaptability and continuous learning. They stay informed about technological advancements, regulatory changes, and market trends. Their ability to quickly adapt to new information and adjust their strategies is a key factor in their success.

A well-defined exit strategy is as important as an entry strategy. Experienced investors plan ahead for different scenarios, setting price targets for profit-taking and stop-loss levels to limit potential losses. Additionally, they regularly review and rebalance their portfolios to align with their changing investment goals and market conditions.

The strategies seasoned investors employ in crypto investing reflect a combination of strategic thinking, risk management, and a deep understanding of market dynamics. These investors have learned through experience that the cryptocurrency market demands a versatile approach that combines patience, analysis, and adaptability. Their successes are a testament to the market's potential when approached with careful consideration and a disciplined outlook.

As the cryptocurrency landscape continues to evolve, these seasoned investors serve as role models for those seeking success in the market. Their strategies emphasize the importance of fundamental and technical analysis, risk management, diversification, and an awareness of market sentiment. By incorporating these lessons into their investment approach, newcomers and experienced investors can navigate the complexities of the crypto market with greater confidence and the potential for long-term success.

CONCLUSION

Recap of Key Takeaways from the Guide

Throughout this comprehensive book, we've embarked on a journey through the multifaceted world of cryptocurrency investments. From understanding the fundamentals of cryptocurrencies to exploring advanced strategies employed by seasoned investors, we've covered various topics designed to equip you with the knowledge and insights needed to navigate the dynamic crypto investment landscape. As we recap the key takeaways from this book, let's reflect on the essential lessons that can guide your path toward successful cryptocurrency investing.

Understanding the Basics:

We began by demystifying cryptocurrencies and blockchain technology. You've learned that cryptocurrencies are digital assets built on secure, decentralized blockchain networks, enabling secure transactions and eliminating the need for intermediaries. This foundational understanding is essential as you delve deeper into crypto investing.

Navigating Blockchain Technology:

Our exploration of blockchain technology illuminated its role as the backbone of cryptocurrencies. You now grasp how blockchain's distributed and immutable nature enhances security and transparency, laying the foundation for innovation and potential disruption across various industries.

Key Terminologies for Success:

To converse fluently in crypto, you've familiarized yourself with critical terms such as wallets, private keys, public keys, and consensus mechanisms. This knowledge enables you to engage confidently in discussions, transactions, and investment decisions.

Diverse Cryptocurrency Landscape:

Our journey into different types of cryptocurrencies unveiled the vast array of projects beyond Bitcoin. From utility tokens to security tokens as well as stablecoins, you've recognized the diversity of available assets and their unique purposes.

Crafting Investment Strategies:

As an investor, knowing your risk tolerance and investment goals is paramount. By assessing your objectives, you're empowered to tailor a strategy that aligns with your aspirations—whether that's a long-term HODLing approach, active trading, or participation in DeFi protocols.

Choosing Exchange Platforms and Wallets:

Selecting the right cryptocurrency exchange platform ensures a secure and user-friendly trading experience. Coupled with knowledge about hot and cold wallets, you've gained insights into safeguarding your investments.

Analyzing Projects and Whitepapers:

In-depth exploration of whitepapers and project concepts empowers you to evaluate various cryptocurrencies' viability and potential impact. Armed with the ability to assess the technology, team, and real-world applications, you can make informed investment decisions.

Assessing Market Data and Sentiment:

Understanding market capitalization, supply, and circulation provides insights into the scope of a cryptocurrency's influence. Combining this knowledge with sentiment analysis equips you to gauge broader market trends and potential investment opportunities.

Evaluating Development Teams and Roadmaps:

By scrutinizing development teams and project roadmaps, you've grasped the significance of a capable team and a well-defined plan. This knowledge allows you to discern projects with a strong potential for growth and success.

Exploring Use Cases and Adoption:

An exploration of use cases and adoption potential illuminated the real-world impact that cryptocurrencies can have. Recognizing their transformative potential across industries positions you to identify projects with a sustainable competitive edge.

Technical Analysis and Trading Strategies:

You've delved into technical analysis, learning to decipher crypto charts and recognize patterns and indicators. This proficiency empowers you to develop trading strategies based on data-driven insights.

Investment Management and Risk Mitigation: Mastering

investment management techniques, such as setting stop-loss and take-profit orders, is crucial to protect your investments and avoid emotional decision-making. This strategic approach safeguards your portfolio from unnecessary losses.

The Power of Diversification:

You've embraced the importance of diversification—a principle that mitigates risk by spreading investments across various assets. This strategy reduces exposure to the volatility of individual assets and contributes to a resilient portfolio.

Understanding News and Sentiment:

Market sentiment plays a pivotal role in influencing cryptocurrency prices. You've learned to approach news and sentiment critically, considering multiple sources and recognizing the psychological factors at play.

Learning from Market Cycles:

Our exploration of past bull and bear markets underscored the cyclical nature of crypto investing. You've internalized lessons about adaptability, patience, and the importance of aligning investment strategies with market trends.

Strategies of Seasoned Investors:

The strategies seasoned investors employ reflect patience, diversification, due diligence, and adaptability. By incorporating these strategies, you're equipped to navigate the complexities of the crypto landscape with greater confidence and resilience.

As we conclude this book, remember that cryptocurrency investing is a continuous learning journey. With the knowledge you've acquired through this book, you're better equipped to make wise choices, control risks, and take advantage of opportunities in the cryptocurrency market. Stay curious, stay informed, and embrace cryptocurrencies' transformative potential to reshape the financial landscape. The future of crypto investing is yours to explore, navigate, and shape—one strategic decision at a time.

Embracing the Evolving Nature of the Crypto Market

The landscape of the cryptocurrency market is dynamic and constantly changing., marked by rapid technological advancements, regulatory shifts, and market sentiment swings. As investors, enthusiasts, and participants in this transformative space, understanding and embracing the fluid nature of the crypto market is essential for navigating change and seizing opportunities. This section delves into the various dimensions of the market's evolution, offering insights into the factors driving change, the challenges posed, and the strategies to capitalize on this ever-changing landscape.

At the heart of the crypto market's evolution lies technological innovation. Blockchain technology, the foundational backbone of cryptocurrencies, continues to undergo advancements that expand its utility and potential impact. From the introduction of smart contracts to the rise of decentralized applications (dApps), these innovations bring real-world solutions to industries such as finance, supply chain management, and healthcare. Embracing this evolution involves staying informed about emerging technologies, recognizing their practical implications, and identifying investment opportunities that align with these advancements.

The trajectory of the cryptocurrency market is significantly influenced by regulatory developments. Globally, governments are attempting to create frameworks that strike the right balance between innovation, consumer protection, and financial stability. As the market matures, regulatory clarity becomes paramount for participants. Embracing the evolving regulatory landscape involves understanding the jurisdiction-specific requirements, staying updated on legal changes, and ensuring compliance with relevant laws. Regulatory certainty not only fosters institutional participation but also enhances investor confidence.

The crypto market's volatile nature is driven, in part, by market sentiment and psychological factors. FOMO (fear of missing out) and also FUD (fear, uncertainty, and doubt) can lead to dramatic price swings. Emotions can cloud judgment, prompting impulsive decisions. Embracing the evolving market involves cultivating emotional discipline, maintaining a long-term perspective, and critically assessing news and sentiment. Investors can make more thoughtful judgments and stay away from emotional responses by understanding the psychological factors that drive market movements.

The pace of change in the crypto market demands adaptability and continuous learning. New projects, technologies, and investment opportunities emerge regularly. Embracing the evolution entails staying curious, engaging in ongoing research, and seeking to understand the nuances of different projects. Flexibility is key; strategies that worked in the past may not apply in a rapidly changing environment. As the market evolves, so too must the strategies employed to navigate it effectively.

The rise of DeFi represents a revolutionary shift in traditional financial systems. DeFi protocols offer lending, borrowing, and trading services without intermediaries, democratizing access to financial services. Embracing this evolution involves exploring DeFi platforms, understanding their risks and benefits, and recognizing the potential to earn passive income via yield farming and liquidity provision. However, it's crucial to exercise caution and conduct thorough due diligence before participating in DeFi projects, given the complexities and risks involved.

The crypto market's evolution is also driven by a community of developers, entrepreneurs, investors, and enthusiasts collaborating to build innovative solutions. Embracing this evolution entails actively participating in industry events, joining online communities, and networking with like-minded individuals. Engaging in discussions, sharing insights, and collaborating on projects can provide valuable perspectives and keep you abreast of emerging trends.

As the crypto market evolves, environmental and social considerations have come to the forefront. Energy consumption associated with proof-of-work blockchains, such as Bitcoin, has raised concerns about sustainability. Innovations like proof-of-stake seek to address these concerns. Embracing the evolution involves being aware of different cryptocurrencies' environmental impact and supporting projects prioritizing sustainability and social responsibility.

The crypto market's evolution introduces both opportunities and risks. Embracing change involves finding the right balance between risk and reward. While the potential for significant gains exists, the market's volatility necessitates careful risk management. Diversification, setting clear investment goals, and employing risk mitigation strategies are crucial to navigate the evolving landscape while safeguarding your investments.

Embracing the evolving nature of the crypto market is akin to embarking on a journey through uncharted waters. The fluidity of the market demands a nimble and informed approach that integrates technological understanding, regulatory compliance, psychological awareness, and adaptability. As the crypto landscape continues to transform, participants who stay informed, remain open to change, and seize opportunities stand to benefit from the potential rewards this dynamic market offers. The journey is not without challenges, but the evolving crypto market promises a future shaped by innovation, disruption, and the resilience of those who navigate its twists and turns with a strategic and informed outlook.

Continuing Your Crypto Education and Journey

Embarking on a journey in cryptocurrency is not a destination but a continuous exploration. The rapidly evolving digital assets and blockchain technology landscape demands an unwavering commitment to education, adaptation, and growth. This section delves into the importance of continuing your crypto education, the avenues available for ongoing learning, and the strategies to navigate the ever-changing world of cryptocurrencies.

In an era of rapid technological advancement, lifelong learning has become a prerequisite for success. With its innovative projects, evolving technologies, and dynamic trends, the cryptocurrency market exemplifies the need for ongoing education. As you traverse this ever-changing terrain, embracing a mindset of constant learning empowers you to remain informed, adaptable, and positioned to capitalize on emerging opportunities.

The landscape of cryptocurrencies and blockchain is marked by constant innovation and transformation. New projects, protocols, and technologies emerge regularly, reshaping the possibilities within the market. Staying informed involves engaging with reputable news sources, following industry influencers, and participating in online forums and communities. Active involvement in these spaces facilitates the exchange of insights, perspectives, and updates on developments that can influence your investment decisions.

The digital age has ushered in a wealth of learning platforms and resources dedicated to educating individuals about cryptocurrencies and blockchain technology. Online courses, webinars, podcasts, and e-books offer structured and comprehensive insights into various aspects of the crypto space. These platforms enable you to learn at your own pace, ensuring that your education remains tailored to your schedule and level of expertise.

Attending industry events and conferences is a unique opportunity to immerse yourself in cryptocurrencies.

These gatherings bring together thought leaders, developers, investors, and enthusiasts, creating an environment conducive to learning, networking, and collaboration. Participating in such events gives you firsthand exposure to the latest trends, innovations, and insights shaping the crypto landscape.

As the cryptocurrency space evolves, acquiring a technical understanding becomes increasingly valuable. Delving into the technical aspects of blockchain technology, consensus mechanisms, and cryptography equips you with a more profound comprehension of the projects you invest in. Resources such as whitepapers, technical documentation, and online tutorials enable you to develop a foundational knowledge of the intricate workings of the technologies that power cryptocurrencies.

The regulatory landscape of cryptocurrencies is subject to continuous change as governments and regulatory bodies establish frameworks to govern this nascent industry. Staying informed about regulatory developments in your jurisdiction is vital to ensuring compliance and safeguarding your investments. Legal courses, expert panels, and regulatory updates help you navigate this aspect of the crypto space, enabling you to make educated decisions that align with the prevailing legal environment.

As you continue your crypto education, embracing ethical and responsible participation in the market is essential. A robust understanding of security best practices, anti-money laundering (AML) regulations, and responsible trading ensures that your engagement in the crypto space contributes positively to the broader ecosystem. Ethical participation fosters trust and legitimacy within the community.

The value of networking and collaboration in crypto cannot be overstated. Engaging with professionals, developers, and fellow enthusiasts creates knowledge exchange, mentorship, and project collaboration opportunities. Networking platforms, conferences, and online communities provide avenues for building meaningful connections that can enhance your understanding of the market and foster collaborative endeavors.

Continuing your crypto education involves adopting a holistic approach that encompasses both technical and fundamental aspects. Balancing your understanding of blockchain technology, market trends, investment strategies, and regulatory dynamics provides you with a well-rounded perspective. This holistic approach enables you to make informed decisions that consider a wide range of factors and variables.

Education is the compass that directs your journey in the constantly shifting world of cryptocurrencies and blockchain. The commitment to lifelong learning positions you as an active participant in a transformative era, where innovation and disruption converge. As you continue your crypto education, remember that your path is dynamic and not fixed. Embrace the excitement of discovery, the challenges of adaptation, and the empowerment of staying informed in a world shaped by digital innovation. Your crypto journey is a testament to your dedication to growth, exploration, and the relentless pursuit of knowledge in the digital age.